This is an easy-to-read guide to practical living in the later years, chock-full of evidence that positive choices in one's day-to-day experience can make a decided difference, and all of life can be marked by growth and joy!

Win and Charles Arn have written a delightful book, filled with practical wisdom on the art of not only enduring, but triumphing in life. Their insights and humor make reading this book great fun.

The Arns' zest for life comes shining through as they present principles of physical and emotional health and longevity helpful to anyone who aims to *live long and love it.*

Win Arn is eminently well qualified to write on aging. He brings to the task a rare combination of personal experience as a senior adult, a background in developing churches in ministry programs, and an ever-expanding knowledge of gerontology. . . . Any church that wants to move out to the growing edge must meet the needs of its aging membership. Books such as this provide valuable resources to assist the church in the challenge.

> David Roddy, director
> Family Life Department
> Florida Baptist Convention

A book of hope and inspiration for senior adults and one that gives vision for ministry in an aging society.

> Joe Bettridge, pastor
> St. Andrew's Presbyterian Church
> Tucson, Arizona

If you are interested in tapping into one of the largest people resources in our society to enable the mission of your church, then this book is required reading for you. It is informative, insightful, challenging, and helpful as you prepare to begin a ministry to older adults.

> Robert Folkers, executive director of ministry
> Northern Annual Conference
> United Methodist Church

Here is some of the best material I have seen that deals with the attitudes of people as they prepare to retire, as well as of those who have already retired. This book is interestingly written, easy to read, and very helpful.

Erwin J. Kolb, retired executive
Lutheran Church, Missouri Synod

A wonderfully comprehensive and detailed look at the joys, the pitfalls, and the solutions to living.

Sid Kullberg
Retired business manager

Live Long and Love It! will inspire and encourage many to realize their potential for productivity.

Dan Dunkelberger
Christian filmmaker and educator

LIVE LONG &LOVE IT!

WIN ARN *with* CHARLES ARN

TYNDALE HOUSE PUBLISHERS, INC.
WHEATON, ILLINOIS

Library of Congress Cataloging-in-Publication Data

Arn, Win.
    Live long and love it! / Win Arn, Charles Arn.
    p.   cm.
    ISBN 0-8423-2116-0
1. Aging—Religious aspects—Christianity.   I. Arn, Charles.
II. Title.
BV4580.A75   1991   91-65585
248.8'5—dc20

98 97 96 95 94 93 92 91
 9   8   7   6   5   4   3   2   1

CONTENTS

Preface

Would you like to live long and love it?

Of course you would! Who wouldn't?

You can! You will find some of the most important secrets to a long and happy life in this book. Few of these secrets are original. For, as Solomon once said, "Nothing is truly new; it has all been done or said before." But I hope these ideas will be as helpful to you as they have been, and continue to be, for me. In fact, the very process of writing this book has not only helped me refocus on these insights, but it has rekindled my own desire to live long and love it!

The turning point for me came just two years ago. Having enjoyed good health and vitality throughout my life, I was surprised one night to find myself in the hospital, the victim of a stroke. While I was recovering, my friend and mentor, Dr. Donald McGavran (ninety-one years old at the time), came to visit me on numerous occasions. Before he left each time he would grip my hand and say, "Win, your best days are still ahead." I was so sick, I believed him!

My brush with death led me to an important discovery. In the hospital, in the recovery center, in community senior activities, and in national seniors organizations, God was ignored. I found a wealth of material on health and nutrition for senior adults. I discovered much information on medicine, housing, and finances for older adults. But little or nothing was available to senior adults that would help them come to grips with spiritual well-being and wholeness.

This realization rubbed against my basic belief and experience that a well-balanced, happy, healthy life has a blend of many aspects, including the spiritual. From my own life experience, I know the benefits of faith in God. Such a faith has been for me—and can be for anyone—a deep well from which to draw strength and courage as the experiences of life hammer upon us. Writing this book was one way for me to address this important aspect of healthy living.

I have tried to bring to these pages a sense of humor, helpful research, and practical discoveries. I hope you will bring to them an open mind, an inquisitive spirit, and a desire to learn. I believe that as you apply what you read, you will reap the harvest of living long and loving it.

I hope you find, as I have found, that your best days are still ahead!

Win Arn, President
L.I.F.E. International

"I DON'T THINK OF MYSELF AS OLD"

1

"The nice thing about birthday shopping for Mother is that she can always use some new hang-gliding accessories."

> **Age doesn't**
> _____
> **matter . . .**
> _____
> **unless you**
> _____
> **are cheese.**
> _____
> *Billie Burke*

*O*ld age begins in the head.

How old you are isn't nearly as important as how old you feel . . . and act and think you are. Research indicates that most healthy people feel about fifteen years younger than their actual physical age. When healthy older people think of "old," they think of someone else.

I have lectured several times to a roomful of people over sixty-five and said, "Look at all those old people." Invariably, everyone turns to see who is walking past the door!

The real question is, as former baseball pitcher

Satchel Paige put it, "How old would you be if you didn't know how old you was?"

Successful aging is typified by the healthy ninety-year-old woman who was meeting with her accountant to review her finances. The accountant, pointing to a considerable sum of money, asked, "What do you plan to do with this fund?" Without hesitation the woman replied, "I'm saving that for my old age!"

Aging begins in the head. When people think of themselves as old, they act old. They take little steps and ease themselves in and out of chairs. They groan when they get up or sit down. Because they feel old, they begin acting old—and they become old.

WHAT IS "OLD"?

Actually, it is becoming increasingly difficult to define *old* or even determine what to call older people. The American Association of Retired Persons (AARP) sets the minimum age for membership as fifty years. Social Security uses the arbitrary figure of sixty-five years. My local newspaper, the daily *Star News*, regularly runs a page for those people fifty years old and above. The restaurant down the street from my home has an entire page on its menu for seniors—anyone over fifty-five years of age.

One good test of getting old is when you find yourself regularly showing off pictures of your grandchildren. Or try the test I read about the other day: While leaning over to tie your shoes, does your mind ask your body, "Is there anything else I should be doing while I'm down here?"

What do we call these people beginning to show increasing amounts of gray hair? No one is quite sure. My own observations, along with marketing research I have read, indicates we do not like to be called "elderly," "seniors," or "golden-agers." Some have tried *whoopies* (short for "well-heeled older people"). Others have tried *opals* ("older persons with active life-styles") and even *grumpies* ("grown-up mature people"). Last week my son-in-law told me the latest term—the "chronologically gifted"! However, none of these have yet taken hold.

Perhaps it has less to do with a numerical age or a designated name than with people's attitudes—how they see themselves and what "old" means to them. A friend who is senior adult pastor at a church in San Diego told me there are three kinds of older adults: the *go-gos*, the *slow-gos*, and the *no-gos*.

WE'VE LIVED THROUGH A LOT!

Perhaps being a senior adult is related more to what we have lived through. We don't know the name of the person who put together the following list, but we identify with it. If you do too, you're probably one of us.

We were here before the pill and the population explosion; before television, penicillin, polio shots, antibiotics, and Frisbees; before frozen food, nylon, Dacron, Xerox, Kinsey, radar, fluorescent lights, credit cards, and ballpoint pens.

When we were young, time-sharing meant togetherness, not computers. A chip meant a piece of wood. Hardware meant hard ware (as in a hardware store), and software wasn't even a word.

We were here before panty hose, drip-dry clothes, ice makers, dishwashers, clothes dryers, freezers, and electric blankets; before Leonard Bernstein, yogurt, Ann Landers, plastic, the forty-hour week, and the minimum wage. We remember when Hawaii and Alaska became states.

We got married first and then lived together . . . how quaint can one be?

Closets were for clothes, not for coming out of. Bunnies were small rabbits, and rabbits were not Volkswagens. We were here before Grandma Moses started painting and Frank Sinatra sang his first song. Girls wore Peter Pan collars and thought cleavage was something butchers did.

We were here before Batman, Rudolph the Red-Nosed Reindeer, and Snoopy; before DDT, vitamin pills, disposable diapers, Jeeps, the Jefferson Memorial, and pizza. We remember when instant coffee, decaffeinated anything, and McDonald's were all unheard of. We thought fast food was what you ate during Lent.

We were here before Boy George, J. D. Salinger, and Chiquita bananas; before FM radios, tape recorders, electric typewriters, word processors, Muzak, electronic music, and disco dancing . . . and that's not all bad!

In our day, cigarette smoking was fashionable, grass was for mowing, Coke was a refreshing drink, and pot was something you cooked in. If we'd been asked to explain CIA, MS, NATO, UFO, NFL, JFK, ERA, or IUD, we would have said: "Alphabet soup!"

We are today's older Americans, a hardy bunch when you think of how our world has changed and what adjustments we have had to make!

One thing is certain, we have had a lot of experience. Bill Cosby tells of one of his daughters asking him on his birthday, "Dad, now that you are fifty, will we have to put you in a home?"

"No," he replied, "Dad is going to hang out for a while so you can have the benefit of all his experience. You see, that's the good thing about getting older—the experience. . . . The problem is, I keep forgetting what that experience was."[1]

A friend of mine told me recently that the advantage of a bad memory is that one enjoys several times the same good things for the first time.

And another insight on how one can look at aging, this one from a bumper sticker: "When we get over the hill, we pick up speed!"

HOW OLD DO YOU FEEL?

A few years ago I was with my friend and colleague Dr. Donald McGavran, who was then well into his eighties. As we were driving, we passed a group of people standing on the sidewalk. Dr. McGavran looked back at them and asked, "Did you see all those old people? They must have been at least sixty-five or seventy years old."

I asked him, "Do you feel old?"

He replied, "No, I feel like I'm forty-five."

While sitting at the Los Angeles airport waiting for a plane, I was thinking about the idea of how old one feels. An older man sat down beside me, looking as if

---

[1]Bill Cosby, *Time Flies* (New York: Doubleday, 1987), 101.

he wanted to talk. "May I ask you a question?" I asked.

"Yes," he replied, "please do."

"How old are you?" I inquired.

"Take a guess," he responded.

"I don't want to play games," I said. "I just want to know how old you are."

"Ninety-four," he answered.

"How old do you feel?" I asked.

"Some days, like one hundred," he said with a twinkle in his eye. "Other days, like twenty-five."

That's a healthy attitude.

Even what we consider "old" is changing, as Charles Schulz, in his *Peanuts* cartoon strip, humorously illustrates. In the opening frame Charlie Brown is talking on the phone: "Well, it sounds like an interesting summer camp, but I haven't decided yet." In the next frame Charlie listens further and responds, "Yes, canoeing, swimming, rock climbing, tennis, hiking, soccer . . . all of those things sound like fun." He pauses. "You are?" Then in the final frame Charlie walks over and tells Lucy, "Grandma says she is going . . ."

Another view of "old" recently appeared in *U.S. News & World Report*. A two-part article entitled "Sixty Something" described Warren Buffett, a man who has built an investment empire by paying close attention to both companies and people. Several years ago he left a ninety-four-year-old woman in charge of one of his companies.

Asked about his decision, he said, "She is clearly gathering speed and may well reach her full potential in another five or ten years. Therefore, I persuaded our board to scrap our 'mandatory retirement at one hundred' policy. . . . Good managers are so scarce, I can't afford the luxury of letting them go just because they have added a few years to their age."[2]

A young-thinking friend of mine, film director Carroll Nyquist, says most of us act as though there were a fence separating us from old age. We always see ourselves as being on the youth side of that fence. Often we go to great lengths to justify positioning ourselves on the favored side, regularly dressing, thinking, and acting young. We are afraid to associate with people who are obviously on the far side of the fence. We fear being identified as "old."

As we grow older, we change the chronological position of the fence. In our twenties, the fence crossing is seen as being around forty. In our forties, the fence crossing is around sixty. As we move into our fifties, the age is seen as around sixty-five or, hopefully, seventy. In our sixties, the fence crossing is seventy-five or even eighty.

[2]David R. Gergen, "Sixty Something," *U.S. News & World Report* (16 April 1990): 64.

WHAT CAUSES AGING?

Researchers are not sure what causes aging. The varied theories on why aging and death occur are fascinating. Here are a few:

One theory of aging suggests that biological change occurs that inhibits a cell's ability to function. When enough cells are inhibited, aging occurs and eventually death results.

Another theory suggests that changes are due to built-in programs in our genes. Just as early growth and development follow a set timetable, so do maturity, aging, and death. If you have long-lived grandparents, you have the right genes.

Another theory suggests that aging is caused as the body's systems are damaged through wear and tear caused by stress, the air we breathe, the unhealthy things we eat, and failure to exercise.

Still another theory suggests that aging is caused by free radicals—chemicals produced in all animals that use oxygen. They bounce around inside body cells, often damaging the vital proteins, fats, and DNA in them. To protect itself, the body uses antioxidants (compounds which block much of this free radical damage). Life can be extended (the theory says) as the body, aided by some vitamins and minerals, produces defenses.

Yet another theory suggests that aging results from

a slow accumulation of damage to the DNA in body cells, causing cells, then body tissue, and finally organs to break down and die.

One theory makes hormones the culprits of physical change. When glands fail to function properly, aging changes begin.

Still another theory of aging relates the changes to the immune system. As we grow older, the immune system becomes less effective and our resistance to bacteria, viruses, and other disease-producing organisms decreases.

So we don't exactly know why we age. Scientists are continuing their studies of aging, seeking to discover which, if any, combination of interventions will extend life.

HOW TO LIVE LONGER

We do know, however, that, as the National Institute on Aging suggests, your chances of living longer and loving it will improve if:

- You have a positive and enthusiastic attitude toward life.
- You don't smoke.
- You eat a balanced diet.
- You maintain your desirable weight.
- You exercise regularly.

- You have regular health checkups.
- You have meaningful relationships with family and friends.
- You keep a balance of sleep, rest, and relaxation.
- You have meaningful work and a purpose in life.
- You drink alcohol beverages only in moderation.
- You practice good safety habits at home, at work, and in automobiles to prevent accidents.[3]

For most people, "old" begins in the head. A fortune cookie I opened put it this way, "Your happiness is intertwined with your outlook in life."

What makes you feel young? Feel good? Identify those things and do them! You will be adding years to your life and life to your years.

Roll back the clock mentally, build happiness into your daily life, and you will benefit! How you think and feel can be the most powerful of all the forces to keep you young and vigorous. That's a characteristic of those who live long and love it.

---

[3]"Help Yourself to Good Health" (Bethesda, Md.: National Institute on Aging), 17.

DISCUSSION QUESTIONS

1. Discuss with some of your friends how old each one feels.

2. Describe a person you know who acts and seems younger than he or she really is. What can you learn from this person?

3. Refer to the National Institute on Aging's suggestions in this chapter for maintaining good health. Identify two that you personally practice and two you feel the need to apply.

ADD YEARS TO YOUR LIFE & LIFE TO YOUR YEARS

2

On his first day of retirement, Carl finds that the experience of "_finally_ getting the driveway resealed" isn't all he dreamed it would be.

> **Life is like a**
> **bicycle—you**
> **don't fall off**
> **until you stop**
> **pedaling.**
> *Claude Pepper*

Rose Blumkin (or Mrs. B, as she is called) started over in business recently. That's not unusual, except that Mrs. B was ninety-six years old.

If your home is near Omaha, you are probably familiar with her name, since Mrs. B is something of a folk hero in those parts. A Russian immigrant, she first went into business in 1937 in the basement of her husband's store. Soon furniture became their main business and Mrs. B the family's main businessperson. By 1983, when Mrs. B sold the Furniture Mart for $60 million to investor Warren Buffett, it had become the largest single furniture outfit in the nation.

When asked why she was starting over in business,

Mrs. B replied that she didn't need the money. Rather, she wanted to get even with her two grandsons who, she said, forced her out as chairperson of the Furniture Mart.

"I wish to live two more years, and I will show them who I am!" said the four-foot-eleven-inch Mrs. B. "I'll give 'em hell."

"Them" refers to grandsons Ron and Irv Blumkin. "They told me I am too old . . . too cranky," she fumed. "I gave my life away for my family. I made them millionaires. I was chairman of the board, and they took away from me my rights. So, I got mad and I walked out. Maybe I have lived too long. Maybe they are tired of me."

Mrs. B did not just walk out. She walked across Jones Street on the west side of Omaha and, in a building the size of a football field, opened Mrs. B's Warehouse to compete with "my high-class grandsons who know only fancy things and who always take vacations."

Mrs. B didn't see the competition as an even match. "They are the elephant, I am the ant," she said. However, before her store officially opened, Mrs. B had grossed $256,000. "I am a fast operator," she said. "Thank God I still have my brains, my know-how, my talent . . . but it's not so easy."

"Anyone who works, lives long," she declares.

Mrs. B puts in fifty to sixty hours per week, darting through the aisles on her golf cart, helping customers and closing sales.

I smile and cheer the pluckiness of this non-agenarian who is willing to roll up her sleeves and say, "It's not over yet. Not by a long shot."[1]

THE VALUE OF MEANINGFUL WORK

Mrs. B was right when she said, "Anyone who works, lives long." In fact, if there is a youth elixir—a magic potion that keeps people young—it is meaningful work. I recently spoke with a life-insurance salesman who told me that the average person dies within seven years after retirement. It is not uncommon for people to die within the first two years.

Richard Sears (of Sears, Roebuck & Co.) began his career in catalog sales when he was working at the local railroad station. A shipment of watches was received by mistake, and he made a deal with the manufacturer to purchase them. His small watch catalog became the beginning of an extraordinary mail-order business. His unusually keen sense of the needs and desires of his clientele made the Sears catalog a household item.

But the revolution in transportation and communi-

[1] ABC's "20/20," 14 June 1988.

cation brought the city closer to the rural areas, and it became evident that Sears would have to establish retail stores to keep up with the rapidly changing face of our country. His superb catalog marketing skills were no longer needed, and he retired. Sears died just a few years later, a man without a mission.

Perhaps you, too, have known people who worked hard, retired, and then promptly died, while others who continued to pursue meaningful work lived on into their eighties and nineties.

In America, we define ourselves primarily by our work. This was once true only of men; now it is increasingly true of women as well. Our work is who we are. We are doctors, accountants, nurses, custodians, teachers, secretaries. Our work enables us to feel part of the total scheme of things. From our work we develop important philosophical, religious, ethical, and vocational values. We are what we do.

Missionary physician Albert Schweitzer practiced medicine well into his nineties. He often said, "I have no intention of dying so long as I can do things; and, if I do things, there is no need to die. So I will live a long, long time." And he did.

Not only does work help us define ourselves, it also becomes the measure of our self-image and self-esteem. And meaningful work helps us to maintain contact with the real world.

THEN COMES RETIREMENT

At a recent AARP convention, Rosalynn Carter told of her mother's retirement after many years of service with the post office. Her retirement took place on Christmas Eve with a wonderful celebration. A few weeks later, Rosalynn found her mother uncharacteristically depressed and in tears. When asked why, she responded, "No one thinks I can do good work anymore."

It seems like such a wonderful dream. No more work. Sleep late. So much time to oneself! But for many people, after retirement something goes terribly wrong. The fishing that one hoped to do becomes boring. The golf game becomes meaningless. The important list of things to do remains undone.

In our video *Live Long and Love It,* a woman remembers her husband's retirement:

Retirement seemed to make him a different person. Before he retired, he was always well organized, never wasted a moment. He always seemed to be in total control. But once he stopped working, he seemed totally lost, like he didn't know what to do with himself.

And that was a problem for me. I mean, I loved my husband very much, but I wasn't used to having him around twenty-four hours a day, and he really got on my nerves.

We had a good marriage. But right after his retirement, things became pretty rocky between us.

Part of the trouble was what he did with his time after retirement, which wasn't much of anything. And what he did do seemed to bore him. Oh, at first he tried to keep himself busy with hobbies and sports, but that didn't last long.

He used to really enjoy stamp collecting and always complained about not having enough time for it. But after he retired, he soon found working with stamps to be boring.

It was the same with sports. For a while he played a lot of golf and tennis. But after a few months he lost interest in almost everything. And it wasn't long before all he was doing was watching television.

He did plan our finances quite well. I have no money problems. But he didn't really do any planning for his retirement. He never found anything to do that seemed meaningful to him.

My husband had an excellent job, and he was good at what he did. But then suddenly he was given his gold watch and forced to stop working. I guess he just didn't feel needed anymore. He died on the day before his sixty-eighth birthday.

Commenting on that woman's experience, psychol-
ogist Eugene Whitney says,

> Unfortunately, this woman's story is very typi-
> cal. Retirement to a life of unending vacation-
> like leisure can be disastrous. I have counseled
> with many retired people who would gladly
> change places with someone who was working
> every day. Some of them would even welcome
> back the pressures and deadlines. Why? For
> one reason. When they worked, even at dis-
> tasteful jobs, they felt needed. They felt their
> lives had purpose and meaning.[2]

RETIREMENT REQUIRES PLANNING

Does that mean we are forever doomed to punch a
time clock in order to survive? No. But it does mean
retirement, to be successful, needs to be planned for,
and we must explore the golden opportunity for
self-expansion. In most cases, this preparation needs
to take place before our actual retirement.

Ken Dychtwald in his book *Age Wave* even suggests that the traditional concept of working and then
retiring is becoming outdated, and that more people

---

[2]Win Arn, producer, *Live Long and Love It:* the video (Monrovia, Calif.: Church
Growth Press, 1990).

are simply changing careers as they live longer. The very concept of retirement, as it now exists, keeps many older people from living productive lives well into later years.[3]

More older Americans are working and bringing their unique skills into the marketplace. The June 1990 *AARP Bulletin* (p. 16) carried the story of Zak and Mitch, identical twins who run a volunteer physics clinic to help students prepare for final exams. Last April, friends held a party honoring the twins on their eightieth birthday. There were many glowing testimonials. In the midst of the celebrating, Zak felt compelled to squelch rumors that he and Mitch would leave the physics clinic at year-end. "We may drop dead, but we won't retire," he said. A relieved cheer went up from the crowd.

A recent issue of *USA Today* featured a cover story with the headlines: "Firms Value Experience, Skill of Seniors." Many companies, the article pointed out, are discovering that senior adults have greater stability, more experience, and stronger customer orientation— qualities that only the school of hard knocks builds into people.

The article further reported that businesses are luring older employees back to work or persuading them

[3]Ken Dychtwald and Joe Flower, *Age Wave: The Challenges and Opportunities of an Aging America* (Los Angeles: J. P. Tarcher, 1989), 175.

to stay longer. Phase-in retirement programs encourage older employees to first try temporary retirement or partial retirement. Aggressive recruiting of senior adult employees—done through mailings, open houses, and informal gatherings—encourages seniors with skills and abilities to consider going back to work. Some companies are providing retirement benefits and no interruption in pensions if retired employees wish to reclaim their old jobs or take new ones within the company.

The article concluded by observing that "while there are still too few companies alive to the possibilities of seniors, and providing attractive incentives, [employing seniors] is part of a trend which we can expect to see more of in coming days."[4]

MAKE YOUR DREAMS COME TRUE

Continuing in an occupation, once you're sixty or sixty-five years old, however, isn't necessarily the only alternative to a boring and meaningless existence. Good planning for your retirement means more than just financial planning. It also means *dream planning*.

Retirement is a chance to do what you've always dreamed about doing. It's the moment you've been waiting for, saving for, and planning for. No more

[4]*USA Today* (13 December 1989): 1.

excuses for why those special things can't be done!

But what is that dream you've had in the back (or front) of your mind for the past few years? An RV trip across the country? Visiting a special place? Learning a new language? Writing a book?

From a physical- and mental-health point of view, it is not only nice to have a dream for your retirement—it is a necessity.

A friend of mine has had for years what he calls his "someday place"—a piece of property in Oregon where someday he is going to build a home and retire. Every summer he camps on the property, cuts back overgrown blackberries, imagines where his house will be built, and visualizes the completed dream. Everyone needs a someday place (or a similar dream for the future). That's part of what keeps a person vital, alive, and looking ahead. Retired people who don't have a dream or purpose for living soon die!

Here's a three-step process for dreaming your way to an exciting retired life. Actually, you don't even have to be retired to discover the wonderful rewards of a dream!

1. Define your dream.
During the coming week, carry a pen and a small tablet around with you. On the front of your tablet write in capital letters: DREAMS.

Inside are your "dream sheets." Put a title at the top of page one that says: "Things I want to do." Title the second page: "Issues I think are important." Title the third page: "People I want to see." Page four: "Skills I want to learn." Page five: "Places I want to go."

Begin by listing anything that comes to your mind. Then, as you go about your daily activities during the week, carry your "dream book" with you and jot down additional thoughts. Talk with friends and relatives about your project and ask if anything you have ever said or done reminds them of something that could be added to your dream sheets.

At the end of the week (or several weeks, if you want to keep your sheets active longer), sit down and review your list. Combine any entries that may overlap. Delete any that seem unimportant after further consideration. Then put your dreams onto one sheet of paper.

Next, select two to four dreams from this list that most energize you. Put a 1 in front of the most important dream, a 2 in front of the next most significant dream, and on through number 4. (Don't go any farther than 4.)

During the next few days, think about these four dreams. Mentally picture yourself pursuing them. What are you doing? How do you feel about it? Who else is involved?

If, after several days, you still feel enthusiastic about these dreams, set a "dream date" for each of your four dreams. Choose when you would like to see that dream become a reality.

Now you can begin to take the next step toward realizing your dreams.

2. Clarify your dream.

Begin with your number-one dream. Take a separate sheet of paper and list all the things that will be involved in reaching your dream. Let's suppose your number-one dream is "visit Spain" and your dream date is two years from now. Visiting Spain is something you've always wanted to do but never seemed to have the time.

Begin a to-do list of all the things that might be involved in visiting Spain. (They don't have to be in chronological order right now.) For example:

To-do List

Learn about places to go and things to do there.
Find out how much it will cost, and develop a
    budget.
Determine who (if anyone) will also go.
Decide when and for how long to be gone.
Visit a travel agent and get brochures.
Go to the library and get books on Spain.
Check the calendar and set tentative dates.

Develop an itinerary.

Write to the Spanish embassy.

Talk with other people who have visited or
lived in Spain.

(Can you think of any others?)

Once you have listed all the things that come to mind
concerning that dream trip, put a completion date for
when each to-do could be accomplished. Keep in
mind your dream date. Your list for the trip to Spain
might look something like this:

Completion Dates (for each to-do)

Learn about places to go and things to do there
(by eighteen months from now)

Find out how much it will cost and develop a
budget (by nine months from now)

Determine who (if anyone) will also go (by six
months from now)

Decide the date to leave and for how long to be
gone (by six months from now)

Visit a travel agent and get brochures (by two
weeks from now)

Go to the library and get books on Spain (by
three weeks from now)

Check the calendar and set tentative dates (by
six months from now)

Develop an itinerary (by twelve months from now)

Write to the Spanish embassy (by two weeks
from now)

Talk with other people who have visited or lived
in Spain (by twenty-four months from now)

The next step is easy. Just put your list of to-dos on a
chart like the one below.

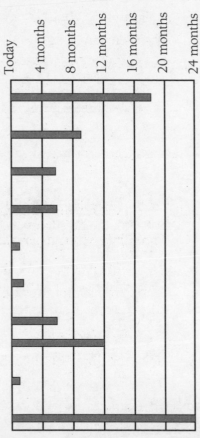

DREAM DATE

	Today	4 months	8 months	12 months	16 months	20 months	24 months
Learn about places to go and things to do there							
Find out how much it will cost and develop a budget							
Determine who (if anyone) will go along							
Decide the date to leave and how long to be gone							
Visit a travel agent and get brochures							
Go to the library and get books on Spain							
Check the calendar and set tentative dates							
Develop itinerary							
Write to the Spanish embassy							
Talk with others who have visited or lived in Spain							

Let's look at another example. Suppose your number-two dream is to learn Spanish.

The first step is to list all the to-dos. Here's what a list might look like:

To-do List

Enroll in a Spanish class at the community
 college
Visit Mexico
Hire a live-in Spanish-speaking housekeeper
Buy some Spanish cassette tapes
(Can you think of any others?)

Next, assign a completion date for each step:

Completion Dates (for each to-do)

Enroll in a Spanish class at the community
 college (within three months)
Visit Mexico (within the next year)
Hire a live-in Spanish-speaking housekeeper
 (within six months)
Buy some Spanish cassette tapes (within two
 months)

Then put these steps on a timeline.

DREAM DATE

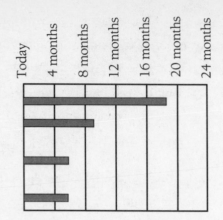

	Today	4 months	8 months	12 months	16 months	20 months	24 months
Enroll in a Spanish class							
Visit Mexico							
Have a live-in Spanish-speaking housekeeper							
Buy some Spanish cassette tapes							

There! See how easy it is? Let's try one more quick one.

Suppose that one of your dream statements was "to make new friends by getting involved in a church-sponsored senior adult program."

This might be your to-do list:

<u>To-do List</u>

Call a variety of churches in the area to find out
what they offer for senior adults (If you are
already involved in a church, help the leader-
ship start a new group for senior adults or
start a L.I.F.E. club. See last page of this book
for information on starting a L.I.F.E. club.)
Select the two churches that most interest you
and find out when their groups meet
Visit both groups

Determine which, if either, group seems to offer
the most benefit to you, and join the group

If this is indeed one of your dreams, assign your own
completion date for each to-do.

The next step is the most fun:

3. Pursue your dream.

An ancient Chinese proverb says that the longest
journey begins with the first step. Many people don't
get anything accomplished because the task seems so
large and insurmountable. But you've already killed
that paper tiger. Just go back to your timeline and look
at when your first to-do should be accomplished. You
might even begin on it today.

In the book *The Courage to Grow Old,* sixty-seven-
year-old Mary Francis Shura Craig, a prolific author of
adult mysteries, reflected on her life. "If I were to do it
all over again, I would study Greek," she wrote. "In
fact, I may anyway."[5]

That's the way to get your dream going. Make a
pact with yourself. Better yet, tell someone else about
your plan. Show them your dream and to-do lists. Ask
them to check up on you occasionally to see how
you're doing with your dreams.

[5]Mary Francis Shura Craig, "A Mosaic of Minutes," in *The Courage to Grow Old,* ed.
Phillip L. Berman (New York: Valentine Books, 1989), 8.

Once you begin, you'll probably find that your dream is much closer than you thought. You may soon be on your way to Spain!

DISCUSSION QUESTIONS

1. Think of long-lived people who had meaningful work and goals. If you meet with a group of senior adults, share illustrations about these people.

2. Ask group members (who are willing) to share a personal dream they still hope to fulfill. If you are not in a group, write one of your own dreams here.

3. Spend approximately ten minutes allowing each group member to complete the steps in "Clarify Your Dream" from this chapter. Ask for volunteers to share their dreams and steps for achieving them. Or take the steps to clarify your own dream—the one you just wrote down.

MAKING HEALTHY CHOICES

3

"I take long walks and get plenty of fiber."

> **If I'd known I**
> _____
>
> **was going to**
> _____
>
> **live this long,**
> _____
>
> **I'd have taken**
> _____
>
> **better care**
> _____
>
> **of myself.**
> _____
>
> *George Burns*

*H*ealth is a major factor for anyone who lives long and loves it because good health makes it much more enjoyable to grow old.

If we had the choice, I'm sure all of us would choose to be healthy. But do we have the choice? In this chapter you are going to meet some people who are convinced that we do. They believe they are healthier because of the life-style choices they have made.

They also believe that the primary reason most people make unhealthy choices is ignorance or a lack of interest.

For the first sixty-four years of my life, I certainly was guilty on both counts. Because my own health

seemed basically good, I had little interest in the subject and paid little attention to either my diet or fitness. My idea of good exercise was a Saturday ride on
my motorcycle, and good nutrition was a thick cut of
red meat with all the trimmings.

Thus I was surprised one night a few years ago to
find myself in the hospital, the victim of a stroke.
Weeks in the hospital, along with regular therapy,
brought a partial return to the life I had previously
lived. But my illness has forced me to pay better attention to both fitness and nutrition.

Nevertheless, I am still no authority, and I feel inad-
equate to write on these topics. Therefore I have asked
my close friend and associate Carroll Nyquist, who has
written and directed many of my films and videos, to
write this chapter.

Carroll is knowledgeable about the basic factors
that affect health and wellness. His grandfather died at
fifty and his father at sixty-three, both from cardiovascular disease. This unfortunate family history has motivated Carroll to do considerable personal study and
research over the past ten years. He has endeavored to
make healthy choices that, he hopes, will counterbal-
ance his hereditary risk factor.

When Carroll first became interested in health
and wellness, he would enthusiastically share his
new insights with me. I must admit that I seldom

listened seriously. The benefit of a low-fat diet and aerobic exercise was not one of my favorite lunch-time topics. But he was a friend, and I'm always polite to my friends. So as he talked about safe cholesterol levels, I enjoyed a three-egg cheese omelet, and I treated him as magnanimously as I would any friend who had become involved in some weird religious or philosophical cult.

However, I now see that the healthy choices Carroll has made seem to be working to his benefit. He is one of the healthiest persons I know. He is almost never sick and seldom suffers even from a cold. Unlike his father or grandfather, his heart is strong, his cholesterol level low, and his blood pressure normal. No matter how much he eats, he remains, in my opinion, disgustingly thin.

Carroll has built up his physical fitness and stamina to where he routinely rides his bicycle a hundred miles in a single day. Surprisingly, he doesn't talk as much about his health habits and convictions as he once did, although I suspect he remains a fervent believer.

Carroll knows what he writes about, and he practices what he preaches. I recommend that you pay close attention to what he has to say in this chapter, because following his suggestions could very well help you to live longer and love it.

To Your Good Health!
by Carroll Nyquist

There's a lot of talk today about extended longevity. Most of us can expect to live longer than people in earlier generations. However, longevity without good health is a dubious blessing.

As a person who is rapidly approaching retirement age, I have long been concerned about how soon, and to what extent, my advancing years will diminish my physical capabilities. I am not at all looking forward to having my mobility limited by a walker or wheelchair.

And most of all, I don't want to follow in the footsteps of my father if I can help it. At age sixty he had his second heart attack, followed by a stroke. This left him bedridden and scarcely able to speak for the three years preceding his death.

Can you or I do anything to increase our chances of remaining healthy and mobile as we grow older? Is good health just a matter of luck? Or is good health a choice over which we have some control? Does the biblical maxim about reaping what one sows apply to health?

For more than ten years, I have avidly read everything I could find on fitness, nutrition, or general health as I have searched for answers to those questions.

The more I have studied, the more it has become clear that personal decision making does play an important role in health. Those daily life-style choices we all make are critical. How physically active do we choose to be? What kind of diet do we choose to eat? How well do we manage stress? By making healthy choices we can improve our chances for combining extended longevity with good health.

I want you to meet some people who have done just that. They have intentionally chosen to be healthy. Now in their seventies, eighties, and even nineties, they are enjoying the benefits of the healthy choices they continue to make. For us they can be beacons of hope illuminating our way to a longer and better life.

MEET LOU ZAMPERINI, AGE 74

During World War II, at the prime of his life, Lou Zamperini spent forty-seven days adrift in a life raft on the Pacific, followed by two and a half years in a Japanese prison camp. These experiences took a devastating toll on his health. Lou recalls feeling that the war took ten years off his life.

Since then, it has been his goal to recover those lost years. To do this, he began making healthy choices in both nutrition and physical fitness. "I've gone into fitness in every way, shape, and form to get those ten years back," he says.

But Lou's approach has been one of moderation. "I'm not a fanatic in any sense," he explains. "I believe that the Bible has been right for thousands of years with the emphasis on moderation. And today doctors, fitness experts, and dieticians are all reverting back to that emphasis—moderation."

Lou believes that "if you do moderate exercise, you can get in the top shape of your life. If you cycle three to six miles every other day, or jog a mile and a half every other day, you'll get in top physical shape—and a marathon runner can't get in any better shape, not for basic health and fitness."

Over the years Lou has engaged in the physical activities he finds most enjoyable—running, hiking, mountain climbing, and snow skiing. Today, at seventy-four, he remains active, managing a senior citizen center. "At work," he says, "I'm up and down the stairs all day long, I put in my walking every day, I bicycle every other day, I'm skateboarding [Lou took up skateboarding several years ago to sharpen his balance for skiing]. And on weekends, I'm hiking and climbing. Then during the winter months I'm skiing as much as I can."

Not only does he have more energy on the ski slopes than most college-age people, he's continually improving. "At seventy-four I'm doing things in skiing I couldn't do when I was sixty-four," Lou says. Lou is an example of how older adults can improve their physical performance, even in their seventies. "Oh, I've got my aches and pains," he admits, "but that doesn't bother me. Not when I'm having fun!"

Meet Hulda Crooks, Age 93

Hulda Crooks, former dietician-researcher at Loma Linda University, believes in the value of making healthy choices, because her choices have drastically changed her life.

Today it is hard to imagine that this vital woman has ever been anything but healthy. But when she was in her early thirties, Hulda's health had become so poor that she was unable to work full time. For years she was, in her own words, "nervous, anemic, and perpetually tired."

Then Hulda married a physician who encouraged her to begin a walking regimen and learn to enjoy nature. The more she walked and smelled the flowers, the more her health improved, until finally she was again able to hold a full-time job.

After her husband's death, Hulda found hiking in the mountains near her home to be excellent grief therapy. At the age of sixty-six, after scaling lesser peaks, Hulda challenged Mt. Whitney—14,495 feet in elevation, the highest peak in the contiguous United States. It is estimated that more than half of those who attempt the climb, regardless of age, give up before reaching the top. But Hulda did not give up. In fact, she has returned more than a dozen times to climb the peak again.

Now in her nineties, Hulda is still climbing. At ninety-one she climbed Japan's 12,388-foot Mt. Fuji, becoming the oldest woman ever to reach its summit. Just six weeks later she made another successful climb to the top of Mt. Whitney.

In the book *Super Seniors,* Hulda gives her philosophy: "When a machine wears out, it can be replaced with a new one. Not so with the human body. Rich or poor, wise or foolish, the limit is one body per customer. No exchanges, trade-ins, or replacements. What's more, only one lease on life is granted. The performance during that lease will, to a large extent, be dependent on the intelligent care given it by the lessee."

Hulda continues: "Plan and put into use a regular exercise program. Set your goal as high as you wish, but work toward it gradually and your body will respond to the utmost of its physiological ability."[1]

MEET "SUPER SENIOR" JACK LALANNE, AGE 75

Jack LaLanne looks twenty years younger than his chronological age. He is perhaps the supreme example

[1]Francis Raymond Line, *Super Seniors* (Irvine, Calif.: Wide Horizons Press, 1989), 87-88.

of an older adult who has benefited from making healthy choices. Jack's appearance is great. His health is excellent, and his physical capability is absolutely amazing.

At sixty, while handcuffed and shackled, Jack swam from Alcatraz Island to Fisherman's Wharf in San Francisco Bay towing a thousand-pound boat. Two years later, for the U.S. Bicentennial Celebration, the sixty-two-year-old fitness proponent, again handcuffed and shackled, swam one-and-a-half miles in Long Beach Harbor towing thirteen boats (representing the thirteen colonies), with seventy-six children as passengers. At sixty-six, Jack swam more than a mile in the coastal waters off North Miami towing ten boats filled with a total of seventy-seven people; it took him less than an hour. At seventy, he swam in Long Beach Harbor towing seventy boats with seventy people for one-and-a-half miles while handcuffed and shackled.

"The most priceless possession we have is our body!" Jack said in a recent newspaper interview. "The worst thing any of us can do physically is to do nothing. The only way you can hurt the body is not to use it."[2] Jack LaLanne seems to be living proof that if you do use it, you don't lose it!

Dr. Robert E. Wear, exercise physiologist at the

---

[2]Bill Billiter, "LaLanne Exhorts Seniors to Tend to Their Bodies," *Los Angeles Times* (20 February 1990): B-1.

University of New Hampshire, agrees completely. "So many people 'rust out' before they 'wear out' because they fail to realize that the human body was made to be used for as long as a person lives," he says.[3]

Perhaps we should listen to Jack LaLanne's suggestion: "In planning for retirement, include your body in the plans."

MEET MAVIS LINDGREN AND CLARA FRAZIER

Lou, Hulda, and Jack began making healthy choices long before they reached retirement age. What about those of us who might be starting now? Is it too late? Are we too old?

To answer that question, I point to additional beacons of hope—Mavis Lindgren and Clara Frazier.

All her life, Mavis Lindgren had suffered from terrible chest colds. At the age of sixty-two she made a life-changing decision to alter her physical life-style. With her doctor's permission Mavis began jogging. At first she could sustain the effort for only a few hundred yards at a time. But she gradually increased her distance until finally she was running an average distance of five miles a day.

Mavis has found that regular exercise makes her feel much better. In the ten years since she started run-

[3]Albert Myers and Christopher P. Andersen, *Success over Sixty* (New York: Summit Books, 1984), 212.

ning, Mavis has not had a single cold and has been sick only once—a bout with the flu that lasted for a day. When she started running, her pulse rate was between seventy-two and seventy-six. Today it is between fifty-two and fifty-six.

In the summer of 1983, Mavis ran the Pike's Peak Marathon eighty-seven minutes faster than she had run it the previous year. She is the world's record holder for her age group, with a time of four hours, twenty-three minutes.

Clara Frazier, now in her eighties, has never run marathons and never intends to. However, she too has learned the benefits of making healthy choices.

Clara recalls returning from a trip to Europe mentally and physically exhausted. "A friend of mine took me to the Manhattan Athletic Club for Women, and it completely changed my life," she says. Clara has been working out ever since. She exercises three times a week, lifting weights, pedaling on an exercycle, swimming, and winding down in the jacuzzi. "I feel great emotionally and physically," she says. "And I just got my driver's license renewed."

Does a woman in her eighties feel some limitations? "I can do anything any thirty-five-year-old woman can do," declares Clara. "My philosophy is to look ahead to tomorrow, to live today, and to learn from yesterday." What does she say to those women and men who panic at reaching forty? "All they need is a little exercise and some love in their lives," she says. "Our bodies are marvelous machines, and with a little care and maintenance, they heal themselves."

It is apparently never too late to benefit from making healthy choices. According to fitness authority and researcher Dr. Lawrence Morehouse,

> Your physiological age is extremely sensitive to the amount of use you make of your body. At a calendar age of sixty, you could be functioning like a seventy-year-old owing to an inactive lifestyle, or you could be going like a significantly younger person because you are active. Conversely, if you are sixty and functioning as if you were seventy, within months you can be well on your way to functioning like a forty-year-old.[4]

WHAT PHYSICAL ACTIVITY IS BEST?

Not too long ago most fitness authorities were insisting that the only way to fitness was to push one's heart rate up to 70 or 80 percent of maximum capacity and keep it there for twenty minutes, three times a week. Only strenuous athletic activities like

[4]Myers and Andersen, *Success,* 219. Mavis and Clara are described on pp. 214-15.

running, high-impact aerobic dancing, and competitive swimming seemed to qualify as beneficial exercise.

As a result, many of us found the idea of exercise far too formidable, and we remained inactive. If ever we were tempted to try working out, we—like Mark Twain—would take a nap until the feeling went away.

Then, a few years ago, exercise physiologists discovered LSD—Long Slow Distance. The idea was that if you exercised for a longer time, at lower intensity, for a greater distance, the benefits to your body would be almost as great as with high-intensity workouts.

With LSD you no longer had to be a super-athlete to exercise. Milder, gentler activities were discovered to be beneficial, even bicycling and walking. Gone were the risks of skeletal and joint damage that had been associated with high-impact activities like running.

At a recent National Institute of Health conference entitled "Exercise in Aging—Its Role in Prevention of Physical Decline," researchers recommended walking as the most effective form of exercise and the only one that can be safely followed throughout one's entire lifetime. Dr. John Pleas, author of the book *Walking* and a personal devotee of this form of exercise, insists that all older adults who can, should walk regularly.[5]

[5] Art Linkletter, *Old Age Is Not for Sissies: Choices for Senior Americans* (New York: Penguin, 1988), 305-6.

Of course, it is smart to check with your doctor before beginning any serious program of physical activity. Whatever your exercise of choice, Dr. Pleas suggests starting gradually. At first, just walk a distance that you find comfortable. Do this three times a week. As you become stronger, increase the length of the walk.

"Exercise should be fun," Lou Zamperini insists. "When I started going to a gym every day, the regimen wasn't really fun. I'd pedal a stationary bicycle and after five minutes look at my watch and feel like I'd been there for two hours. Then I started to take my bike out on the street, and I could ride for hours and feel like it was five minutes. I often ride my bicycle up the canyon and all of a sudden find I've been riding for an hour and a half and I'm late for dinner.

"Get involved with a sport you enjoy—any sport where you can go out there and play an hour or two and don't want to stop when the time's up."

Porter Shimer, former editor of the *Executive Fitness Newsletter,* suggests that we need to redefine exercise to include any kind of physical activity. In his view, energy spent mowing the lawn counts as much as that used on a three-mile run. And the exertion you use playing a game of softball or volleyball is just as good as that spent on the rowing machine, even if your heart doesn't pound the whole time.

Porter sees household chores as a valid fitness activity. Instead of working out, he recommends working around the house. According to Porter's thesis, any activity that burns calories counts. He would include digging in the garden, raking leaves, grocery shopping, walking the dog, playing with your children or grandchildren, fixing the car, or even dancing.[6]

Porter's idea is supported by recent research. A 1987 study at the University of Minnesota found that men who got an average of forty-seven minutes a day of exercise—mainly by mowing the lawn, gardening, and working around the house—had markedly fewer heart attack deaths than did sedentary men.

So the good news is that your healthy choices for physical activities are not limited to jogging or joining a gym—unless that is your preference. You don't have to run marathons. You don't have to spend an hour a day pumping iron. All that's needed is to choose an active over a sedentary life.

The important key is to avoid assuming that getting older means we have to slow down, because slowing down—becoming less and less active—is a sure way to lose fitness and mobility. Unlike most machines, our remarkable bodies were made to grow

[6]Porter Shimer and Bryant Stamford, *Fitness without Exercise: The Scientifically Proven Strategy for Achieving Maximum Health with Minimum Effort* (New York: Warner Books, 1990).

stronger with use. And the more actively we use our bodies, the better they will work for us.

But—and this is critical—you can't keep healthy through physical activity alone. There is another category of healthy choices. What we choose to eat is also very important!

MEET MARION AND MYRON PINKSTON

Marion and Myron Pinkston are not world-class athletes. Neither are they fitness fanatics. In fact, the only exercise Myron gets is gardening and climbing the hill to his workshop. But they, too, are beacons of hope for us all. Both are fit, and their health is exemplary.

Marion and Myron are both eighty years of age. They are hardly ever sick. Myron hasn't suffered from a cold or headache in five years.

So far, Myron has experienced none of the typical medical problems that usually occur as the body ages: high blood pressure, elevated blood cholesterol, slower metabolism, stiff joints, gum disease, bone shrinkage, reduced mental acuity, or digestive problems.

Marion's health is also good. She has a strong pulse, ideal blood pressure, low cholesterol, and a straight back. She shows no sign of osteoporosis, even though 90 percent of all women her age in our country suffer from this disease which makes bones brittle and often curves the spine.

Why are the Pinkstons so healthy? Besides the fact that they have remained active, the quality of their diet is an important factor.

Marion not only cooks all of their meals but manages to prepare many special foods like her high-fiber "health loaf" bread, which contains freshly ground wheat and rye flours, oats, wheat germ, honey, marmalade, almond extract, and nonfat milk. Good nutrition is important to Marion. She studies publications that provide health information and clips appropriate recipes to include in their daily menus.

This couple's diet is low in fat and high in fiber. "The fiber fad made a lot of sense," says Marion, "and changed my approach to menu planning." She carefully watches their fiber intake and makes sure they eat at least four servings of fruits and vegetables every day.

Some people ask, "What is fiber?" It is that part of many foods which is non-digestible and sometimes referred to as "bulk." Although technically not a nutrient, fiber is an important dietary element especially vital to proper intestinal function. Eating foods with high fiber gives one a feeling of fullness with less calories, an advantage for anyone wanting to eat less. Certain kinds of fiber play a helpful role in reducing cholesterol levels. Low-fiber diets are associated with chronic irregularity, certain forms of cancer, diverticulosis, and intestinal disease. To boost fiber in your diet, eat more whole grains, bran cereals, legumes (such as dried beans), fruits, and vegetables.

The National Cancer Institute estimates that 35 percent of all cancer deaths in the United States, including lung, breast, colon, rectum, prostate, and bladder cancers, can be traced to poor dietary habits. As a result, the National Academy of Sciences, the United States Department of Agriculture, the American Cancer Society, and the Health Services Department have all increased their recommendation from four servings of fruits and vegetables per day to five. (One serving is equivalent to one whole piece of fruit or one-half cup cut-up fruit, one-half cup cooked vegetable, one cup leafy greens, or one-quarter cup dried fruit.) [7]

HOW IMPORTANT IS DIET?

There's so much confusion and misinformation about food and diets that many of us feel it's easier to be ignorant about nutrition and simply eat whatever tastes good. Depending upon our acquired tastes, such a practice might be very good—or it might be very bad.

[7]Toni Tipton, "Nutritionally Speaking," *Los Angeles Times* (16 August 1990): H-54.

Let me suggest an oversimplified approach to healthy eating and encourage you to do what the Pinkstons do:

- Avoid high-fat foods
- Indulge in high-fiber foods
- Minimize meats
- Maximize fruits, vegetables, and whole grains

If you follow these simple guidelines you can improve your health without ever having to learn about serum cholesterol, saturated fats, or other nutritional complexities.

Such a dietary approach has proven health benefits. It reduces obesity, it is beneficial to diabetics, it reduces risks for some forms of cancer, and it minimizes the possibility of arterial diseases that result in heart attacks and strokes.

We know that fat is the villain that helps clog our veins and arteries. According to Porter Shimer, "The best way to keep fat out of your arteries is by keeping it out of your mouth!"[8]

Remember that what you eat is far more important than how much you eat. If you choose to eat high-fat foods, no quantity is small enough to be healthy. But if you choose to eat low-fat, high-fiber foods, you can

[8]Shimer and Stamford, *Fitness,* 87.

usually eat as much as you want and at the same time maintain or improve your health.

All the people you have met in this chapter are concerned about good nutrition. Jack LaLanne says, "Fat is F—A—T. It's Fatal, Awful, Terrible." He also recommends a good breakfast. "Would you get your dog up in the morning and give him a cup of coffee, a cigarette, and a doughnut? Of course not. You'd kill the dog if you did that." And Jack opposes processed foods. "I know many of you are confused about nutrition," he says. "I'm going to make it easy for you—if it's man-made, don't eat it."

Hulda Crooks, the ninety-three-year-old mountain climber, has thrived on a low-fat, high-fiber, vegetarian diet. "Learn to enjoy good food, simply prepared," she advises. "No type of flesh food is required for good nutrition; if it is used, lean is preferable."

Lou Zamperini recommends moderation in eating as well as in exercise. "I don't go overboard on any particular food," he explains. "Basically, I eat mostly vegetables, fruit, and whole grain cereals." He is moderate on meat and eats primarily fish and chicken.

So when you make your next mealtime choice, remember to avoid high-fat foods, indulge in high-fiber foods, minimize meats, and maximize fruits, vegetables, and whole grains.

And remember the activity connection. Exercising

has an effect similar to turning up the thermostat on your home furnace. Active persons burn their body fuel at a faster rate. This allows them to eat more without weight gain. For maximum health, combine good nutritional choices with an increased level of physical activity. You can't improve your health with either nutrition or exercise alone. You need both!

Choose health!

A Brief Comment about Smoking

I am assuming that you have already made the critical health choice of not smoking and that it is not one of your life-style problems. It doesn't seem as if it should be necessary to repeat any of the well-known facts about the grave dangers of smoking tobacco. Not only does smoking cause lung cancer, but it significantly increases the risk factor for virtually all the major degenerative diseases such as heart attack, stroke, and maturity onset diabetes. If tobacco continues to be a regular part of a person's life-style, no amount of exercise or good nutrition can adequately compensate for the damage it causes.

If you are addicted to this destructive habit, I suggest that you consider one of the many quit-smoking programs or plans that are available. By all means get some help and quit. You'll be glad you did. One of the healthiest choices a person can make is not to smoke.

SOWING AND REAPING

My father grew up on a farm and knew a lot about
planting and harvesting. As a minister, he frequently
used agricultural examples to illustrate the meaning of
the scriptural principle "Whatsoever a man sows, that
shall he also reap."

But somehow he never connected that principle
with his personal health. He was overweight. His diet
was poor (ice cream was his favorite food). His job
was stressful. His blood pressure was high. Aside from
a very occasional and leisurely game of golf, he was
generally inactive. And his family history was certainly
unfavorable, since his own father (my grandfather)
died at age fifty of arterial disease.

Ultimately my father reaped the heart condition he
had sown and tragically died at age sixty-three.

However, in my father's defense, let me say that neither he nor his doctors had the benefit of the information we have today. Forty years ago there was little
understanding that being overweight and eating a
high-fat diet were risk factors for heart disease. It was
not known that moderate exercise was beneficial for
avoiding and recuperating from heart attacks.

After my father's first heart attack, he was advised
by his doctors—as was the standard practice at the
time—to limit all his physical activity. Some minimal
dietary changes were suggested but not stressed. So

actually, my father's problem was not that he made bad choices but that he had bad information. He obediently followed his doctors' instructions and in five years had another heart attack, followed by a stroke, followed by three miserable, helpless years in a nursing home, followed by death.

If my father and his doctors had known then what we know today, I am convinced that the final chapter of his life would have been quite different. He was a very disciplined man. Had he understood the importance of physical activity and good nutrition, he would have radically changed his life-style. And had he done so, he might still be alive.

Unlike my father, I know better. I have acquired excellent health information and would be a fool not to use what I know, unless I want to follow in my father's footsteps.

What have I done about my own health?

For a long time I did absolutely nothing. Then about ten years ago, motivated by what happened to my father, I began reading about heart disease and the latest medical discoveries. In time, that information provided guidelines for changing my sedentary life-style and poor eating habits. I began eating food that was lower in fat and higher in complex carbohydrates—more fruits, vegetables, and whole grains. And I increased my physical activity level by riding a bicycle.

In the six or seven years since, I have lost excess weight and increased my fitness. I could never have done this without choosing an activity that I enjoy—bicycling. By gradually increasing the frequency and extending the distances I ride, I have been able to achieve what Lou Zamperini calls "top fitness for good health." No, I could never qualify to ride in the Tour de France; but I can easily handle day trips of seventy-five to one hundred miles and enjoy them. And I have more energy for my daily responsibilities.

I now have more options for doing fun things that require fitness. I am able to do some fulfilling and physically challenging activities, including hiking to the summit of Mt. Whitney.

What benefits have I experienced? I have already lived beyond the chronological ages at which my grandfather died from a cerebral hemorrhage and my father had his first two heart attacks. Of course, I have no guarantee that I will never have problems with cardiovascular disease. But because I make healthy choices, I am now considered to be at low risk.

Check with me in another ten to fifteen years and see how I'm doing. If the choices are still mine to make, I expect to be riding my bicycle and eating a low-fat, high-fiber diet.

CHOOSE LIFE!

For centuries, people have risked their lives and fortunes to find the fountain of youth. Yet you and I can look and feel younger with little risk or expense. All we have to do is make a few healthy life-style choices.

If you want to add years to your life and life to your years, then choose to be active rather than to sit around. And watch what you eat. That's the challenge people like Lou Zamperini, Hulda Crooks, Jack LaLanne, Mavis Lindgren, Clara Frazier, and Marion and Myron Pinkston give to us. Even if we haven't the slightest interest in towing boats in the San Francisco Bay, running the Pike's Peak Marathon, or climbing Mt. Fuji, I think we are all interested in functioning below our chronological age.

Some older adults are vital and vigorous, while others have difficulty getting up out of their chairs and walking from place to place. For most of us, the difference is the result of life-style choices.

What's your choice?

"I have set before you life or death. . . . Oh, that you would choose life"![9]

[9]Deuteronomy 30:19, *The Living Bible.*

DISCUSSION QUESTIONS

1. Try to recall what you ate for your most recent meal. Discuss whether you made healthy choices.

2. Drawing from either personal experience or observation of others, identify ways that exercise can be both fun and beneficial.

3. Identify one person in this chapter who might qualify as your fitness hero. Why? How could you take steps to follow this person's lead?

MAKING CHANGE
WORK FOR YOU

4

"This is nearly awful enough to be considered a personal growth opportunity."

Nothing
endures
but change.

Heraclitus

An old Chinese parable tells of a farmer who had but one house, one horse, and one son to help him cultivate his little plot of ground. One day his only horse ran away. His neighbors quickly gathered to console him. But he said, "I don't know that it is so bad."

A few days later, the horse came back with two other horses following him. The farmer's neighbors quickly came to congratulate him on his good fortune. But the wise farmer said, "I don't know that it is so good."

Not long after, his only son broke his leg trying to train the new horses. Immediately the neighbors sympathized. But the farmer once again remarked, "I don't know that it is so bad."

Shortly thereafter, the army came through, taking all the young men worthy of battle. When they came to the farmer, they said, "We want your son for a suicide mission." The farmer said, "He is over there with a broken leg." The soldiers said, "A broken leg? Then we can't use him," and went on.

The story could go on and on. But the clear lesson is that most of us spend our lives passing immediate judgment about what is good and bad for us, failing to recognize that change is the only constant in life. Good and bad are endlessly intertwined. They can seldom be evaluated in the here and now. In my own experiences of change, I have found this Bible verse very helpful: "We know that in all things God works for the good of those who love him, who have been called according to his purpose."[1]

Senior adults who live long and love it realize there will be changes in their life situations. These people creatively and positively respond to such changes by using them as growth opportunities.

The fact is that there *has been* change, there *is* change, and there always *will be* change. Indeed, as the ancient truism says, "Nothing endures but change."

[1]Romans 8:28, New International Version.

Those who live long and love it are not those whom change has somehow passed by. They are those who have learned to cope with change as it comes.

KINDS OF CHANGES

What are these changes that we can expect or perhaps have already experienced? I have found the Holmes-Rahe Stress Scale helpful. It was originally developed by two physicians at the University of Washington in an effort to see if there were common denominators among people who had heart attacks.

The physicians began by identifying various stress events that happen in one's life; then they ranked them in order of severity or intensity of effect. When they looked for relationships between heart attack victims and these stress events, they observed a strong correlation. Stressful life events often resulted in debilitating physical consequences.

On the Holmes-Rahe Scale, more than half the stress events typically occur in the lives of persons over fifty years of age. The older an individual becomes, the oftener he or she experiences life-changing events. These events, however, should not necessarily be seen as negative. They can provide windows of opportunity for positive change. They can help us grow and move forward in our lives.

Below is a modified version of the Holmes-Rahe Stress Scale, which I have developed with Dr. Rahe's permission. This scale adds additional life events that often occur among senior adults and assigns them a relative numerical severity. If one or more of the high-scored events (or a combination of events with lower scores) has occurred in your life recently, and if you are feeling particularly "stressed out," you would do well to consult your physician.

Looking at the more significant events topping this list of life-transition experiences, one may ask, "Have we been painting much too rosy a picture of retirement and getting old?" Even though we live longer and better nowadays, and even if we take excellent care of ourselves, sooner or later things can get pretty tough.

At times life can knock us flat and take the wind right out of our sails. The loss of a loved one, the discovery of a life-threatening disease—these are some painful transitions in life of which we all are aware. Those changes, whether they happen to us or to those around us, put a lump in our throat, a tear on our cheek. Even the great apostle Paul said we can be knocked down, though we may not be knocked out.[2]

[2]See 2 Corinthians 4:9.

ARN SENIOR STRESS SCALE

ADULT AGE LIFE EVENT	RANK
1. Death of a spouse	100
2. Divorce	73
3. Move to nursing home	70
4. Marital separation	65
5. Death of a close family member	63
6. Major physical problems	53
7. Marriage/remarriage	50
8. Realizing one has no plans/dreams	47
9. Financial loss of retirement money	47
10. Forced early retirement	46
11. Unable to maintain driver's license	45
12. Marital reconciliation	45
13. Retirement	45
14. Spouse confined to retirement home	45
15. Change of health of family member	44
16. Gaining a new family member	39
17. Change in financial state	38
18. Death of a close friend	37
19. Difficulty getting medical insurance	36
20. Change in number of arguments with spouse	35
21. Mortgage over $50,000	31
22. Foreclosure of mortgage or loan	30
23. Feelings of not being needed	29
24. Feelings of lack of purpose	28
25. Outstanding personal achievement	28
26. Wife begins or stops work	26
27. Significantly decreased contact with children/friends	25
28. Revision of personal habits	24
29. Significantly less contact with support groups	24
30. Trouble with the boss	23
31. Minor physical problems	20
32. Change in recreation	19
33. Change in church activities	19
34. Change in social activities	18
35. Mortgage or loan less than $50,000	17
36. Change in sleeping habits	16
37. Change in number of family get-togethers	15
38. Change in eating habits	15
39. Vacation	13
40. Christmas	12
41. Minor law violation	11

WHY SUFFERING?

During my forty years in the ministry, my work has brought me into contact with many people who, when facing times of great transition, often asked the question, Why me? The *why* question of suffering is very difficult, if not impossible, to answer. Numerous books have been written on the subject. Philosophers and theologians have struggled with the question for centuries. Still, the *why* question will not go away.

I spoke earlier of my wise old friend, Dr. Donald McGavran. I recall one day driving with him to a seminar. His wife was bedridden with encephalitis. He was suffering from cancer. Two years earlier a serious eye problem had left him unable to see clearly enough to read. "You have given most of your life in God's service," I said. "You were a missionary, like your father and grandfather. Now there seem to be so many things making your life difficult. How do you explain all that?"

Dr. McGavran paused for a moment, and then said, "Mary and I have enjoyed many, many years of good health. Problems come to Christians and non-Christians alike. It rains on the just and the unjust, without distinction. Looking back, I have much to be thankful for."

I recall my own experience following my stroke. As I lay helpless on my hospital bed, there were many frightening, soul-searching moments. Would I recover and continue to be productive? Or would I spend the rest of my life as an invalid, a burden to my family and friends? I did not know, yet through these trying times I was sustained and comforted by the presence of the Lord. I knew that whatever might be ahead, I was not alone.

Much of the *why* question can be answered only by faith, taking a longer-term view of our lives—one we often cannot see from day to day. I find helpful the illustration of a person standing on the bridge of a ship in the open sea. It is impossible, by looking forward, to tell what direction the ship is moving, whether it is turning or traveling a straight course. Only by looking back at the wake on the ocean can one see the direction that the captain is guiding the ship. So it is in life. When we look back and see how God has been present in our lives, we are assured that he has no intention of leaving or forsaking us.

Although the human spirit has a great need to understand, or at least to make some sense of suffering, we will never have satisfactory answers to these difficult questions short of eternity. Life is like a beautiful, complex tapestry: we now see only the underside of confusing threads, knots, and jumbled colors. But one day, when the tapestry is turned over for us, we will view it from the front side, and the exquisite beauty of purpose and order and design will become clear.

LOOKING FORWARD

So we can expect change. Change is sometimes welcome, sometimes dreaded. But healthy senior adults realize that it is inevitable. And the best approach is to refrain from labeling it good or bad.

We may not know *why*, but we do know this: an optimistic, forward-looking, courageous attitude toward the future is the secret to dealing with change. By contrast, when people begin looking backward to their life before the change, it is the beginning of the end.

In the book *The Courage to Grow Old*, prominent men and women reflect on growing old. Chapter after chapter rings with that common thread of optimism. You can sense it in the titles: "One More Adventure," "Higher Mountains Yet to Climb," "No Time for a Rocker," "Always Ahead."[3]

These people are still looking forward. That's what healthy seniors do. They look for—indeed, actively search for—the good that tomorrow will bring. It reminds me of a little poem my mother used to recite to me:

> The covered wagon rolled and pitched
> Along the prairie track.
> One sat looking forward,

---

[3] Phillip L. Berman, ed., *The Courage to Grow Old* (New York: Valentine Books, 1989).

While one sat looking back.
One scanned the vast horizon
For a bright and better day,
While the other watched the fading road,
'Til it, too, slipped away.
The covered wagon rolled and pitched
Along the prairie track.
One sat looking forward,
While one sat looking back.

Author unknown

FACING CHANGES

As you experience these inevitable changes, let me share with you four suggestions I believe you will find helpful. In fact, you can begin practicing them even before you need them.

1. Keep searching for the good.

We've all heard the question, Do you see the cup half-full or half-empty? People who see the cup half-full are able to handle change much better. They have a positive mental attitude. The apostle Paul, as we saw earlier, took the view that "in all things God works for the good of those who love him, who have been called according to his purpose." Work on developing an outlook on life that says, with the poet Robert Browning, "The best is yet to be."

2. Count your blessings.

My daughter has a friend with cerebral palsy. She spends most of her waking hours in a wheelchair. When she does walk, it is awkward, uncoordinated, and sad to watch. Her speech is slurred, her eyes crossed, her face contorted. But she just completed her bachelor of arts degree summa cum laude, and she is optimistically looking for a job. She told me the other day, "I'm luckier than a lot of people. I could be paralyzed." When change happens to you—and it will—remember the things you do have, and count your blessings.

3. Focus on the long term.

Remember the parable of the Chinese farmer. One of its lessons is that time is the great healer. What seems unbearable today will, I guarantee you, become manageable with time—perhaps even desirable. One of my favorite songs we sing in church ends with the phrase, "The darkest hour means dawn is just in sight."

4. Get out of yourself.

The more we think about ourselves and our own problems, the more miserable we become. The more we focus on helping others solve their problems, the happier we become. Often the best approach to handling change is to spend our time and energy helping someone else. In losing ourselves in a greater cause, we can actually find ourselves.

Helping Friends Through Change

Most likely your friends and family will also experience change during the coming years. What a wonderful and very important opportunity you have to help them through these important transitions!

Many people feel awkward around others who are experiencing pain, grief, or suffering. However, in life's dark moments you can be a beacon of hope and love. Here are a few suggestions to help you be more effective in these important times:

Be a good listener.

The first funeral I conducted after graduating from seminary taught me an important lesson. The service had ended and the mourners had gone, except for the husband of the deceased. He walked to the front, stood by the casket, and motioned me to join him. As I approached, my mind was racing. What would I say? How would I comfort this man? But before I could speak he started talking. He wanted to tell me about the good life they had shared together. He wasn't seeking words of comfort but ears of understanding. I gained a great insight that day: empathetic listening is a most effective means of support, help, and love.

Identify ways you can help.

People facing change frequently have very tangible
needs you can help meet. Does the person need
transportation? Are meals a problem? What about
medical appointments? Some churches that carry on
an effective senior adult ministry have developed ways
to help people through these transition events. I was
recently conducting a seminar in a Lutheran church.
Across the hall, a support group was meeting for those
who had suffered strokes. There were more than
twenty people in the group, and only a few of them
had been previously involved in the church.

Remember that what you do is as important as what you say.

Often just being there says more than you will
ever be able to verbalize. And that, in itself, says a
great deal. As you do share together, however,
remember some don'ts to avoid in conversation with
those in pain or grief: "I know exactly how you feel";
"Call me if you need something"; "You're lucky you
had so many years together"; "You'll get over it soon."
Things you can say are: "I'm sorry"; "I'd like to help";
"May I bring over a meal we can share together?" "Let's
go for a walk."

Encourage the person to begin getting out of himself or herself.

In the *Reader's Digest,* a sixty-two-year-old woman recently told her painful story of the loss of her husband after forty years of marriage. He had been suddenly and tragically killed in a car accident on his way home from work. As a homemaker, she had looked forward to 5:30 in the afternoon when the front door would open and the booming voice would call out, "I'm home!"

In the months following the funeral she increasingly withdrew from her social and family life and became a recluse in her own house. The worst part of the day for her became 5:30 in the afternoon. She tried not to think about it, but that only made it worse.

Finally, after her physical and mental health had deteriorated for a year, her physician suggested she try working with people who were worse off than she. So, with more desperation than enthusiasm, she began leading a group of handicapped young people on walks through the nearby park. As she spent more and more time with them, she found herself thinking less and less about her own problems. The walks happened to be in the afternoon. One day she realized that no longer was 5:30 the worst time of the day. It was again the time she looked forward to all day long.

One of the best ways you can show love for others is by recognizing changes when they take place in their lives and responding in a loving and understanding manner.

Change is part of our human experience. It always will be. Some people see change as an unwanted intrusion in life. It makes life more difficult, less enjoyable, and undesirably complicated. Such people respond to change with anger, fear, annoyance, or retreat.

Others, however, see their new situation through optimistic eyes of expectation. Change often begins a wonderful new part of their lives. The same event, for these forward-looking people, becomes an opportunity to grow and expand.

A SILVER LINING

On a trip to Colorado, I learned a wonderful true story that shows how change can be a positive or negative factor in our lives, depending entirely on how we view it. The story took place over a hundred years ago, high in the Rocky Mountains.

"Gold! Gold!" The shouts echoed through the hills near the town of Leadville, Colorado, during the 1860s. A gold rush was on, and men by the thousands searched for their fortunes in the bottom of their panning tins. But a decade and a half later, the ruins of Leadville told of a boomtown gone bust. In the nearby

California Gulch (named after the gold dreams of the forty-niners out West) only remnants of abandoned cabins and sluice boxes remained. A few diehard prospectors stayed around, rewashing the gulch gravel for pocket money.

The California Gulch had a nasty reputation among the veteran prospectors. "It's that black sand!" they complained. "It gums up the riffles in sluice boxes. It fills panning holes we dug the day before. It ruins good clothes."

The black sand seemed to cover every gold nugget with grime and grit. It made a mockery of any attempt to find one's fortune. The prospectors that had come to Leadville in great numbers had soon left. Discouraged, they cursed the black sand and moved on in search of easier streams to riches.

Then William H. Stevens and Alvinus B. Wood came upon the remnants of abandoned mines and sluice boxes in the California Gulch. Convinced there was still gold beneath the surface, these two mining men began buying old claims. Initial gold finds increased their efforts and heightened their expectations. But soon they, too, encountered the problems earlier prospectors had faced. The black sand forced delays and hampered progress until it appeared the entire project would fall victim to the wretched grit.

One day Stevens decided to send a sample of "that

black stuff" to the East Coast for analysis. To their surprise, the men learned the black sand was lead carbonate—loaded with silver!

Stevens and Wood staked lode claims throughout the California Gulch and opened Rock Mine, the first producing silver mine in the district. They became fabulously rich in a few short years.

The black sand, which miners and prospectors had cursed as an abominable intrusion in the pursuit of their gold dreams, contained wealth beyond their wildest imaginations! The sandy California Gulch yielded a pittance in gold but a fortune in silver.

I urge you to look at the changes that have happened and will happen to you and ask, Can I see the possibilities and opportunities in my new life situation? Those people who live long and love it search out the exciting riches that change has made possible.

DISCUSSION QUESTIONS

1. If you meet with a group, ask participants to share an experience which seemed bad at the time but turned out to be good.

2. Share a time in your life when a change took place, and tell how you coped with it.

3. What change do you fear most? How have others dealt with a similar change?

4. Consider Robert Browning's oft-quoted words, "The best is yet to be." What did he mean? Did he know what he was talking about?

DEVELOPING COURAGE

5

"Nothing much scares me after a depression, three wars, five kids, and fourteen seasons of 'Dallas.'"

> **What a**
> _____
> **new face**
> _____
> **courage**
> _____
> **puts on**
> _____
> **everything!**
> _____
> *Ralph Waldo Emerson*

J ump . . . Go ahead . . . Jump!"

There I was, fifty feet above the crowd staring up at me. I was balancing on a small two-foot-square platform, preparing to jump. The people below were shouting, "Go on! You can do it!"

I was terrified.

The dictionary defines courage as "the mental or moral strength to venture, persevere, and withstand danger, fear, or difficulty."

I certainly wasn't feeling very courageous that day. The young people in a youth circus had convinced me to climb a rope ladder to the top of their high trapeze and try swinging across to the other side. How did I get into such a strange predicament? I was, at that particular time, wondering exactly the same thing.

This talented group was the cast for a film I was producing. One afternoon while waiting for the cameraman, a young man pointed to the high trapeze and said to me, "Hey, why don't you try it? You'll like it!"

I quickly changed the subject. I knew I wouldn't like it at all. But others in the group heard the challenge and joined the growing chorus: "Try it . . . try it . . . try it!" Eyeing the large safety net under the trapeze, I cautiously replied, "Well, why not?"

Mustering all my courage, I slowly and carefully began climbing the small rope ladder. Twenty feet . . . thirty feet . . . thirty-five feet . . . forty thousand feet . . . fifty thousand feet! Finally I reached a minuscule platform that seemed miles above the group below. My palms were sweaty and beads of perspiration covered my forehead. I looked down.

The once-large safety net had shrunk to unbelievably small proportions. A slight breeze had come up, causing the platform to sway gently back and forth and the wires to sigh in the wind. The young people were looking up and encouraging me: "Go ahead. You can do it!"

I took the trapeze bar in my hands, steadied my shaking knees, and prepared to jump. Across from my platform, a youth was ready to send an empty trapeze bar toward me. I was supposed to jump from one bar to the other. I gripped the bar again and went swinging into space.

Flying through the air, I made three important discoveries:

First, you can't hold onto your own bar and expect to grab hold of the other. You must let go with both hands and leap.

Second, it's frightening to let go of your only security.

Third, you don't have forever to make up your mind. "Jump! Go ahead. Jump!"

On the third swing, I did! Flying through the air, I let go and grasped the other bar at just the right moment. I went swinging to the other side and was pulled safely to the platform.

Amid the applause and cheers from the youth below, I knew that, to them, I had shown considerable courage. I suppose I had. For, while most of the kids in that youth circus wouldn't have thought a second time about climbing the ladder, it took courage for me to do what I had just done.

Courage takes many forms. We face the need for courage on an almost daily basis. Courage comes particularly into play the first time we attempt a task or face a strange situation.

When I was in Iran some years ago, I saw how Persian rug dealers laid their carpets on the sidewalk.

Some even put them in the street during their business hours. I asked a friend why they would want to ruin their expensive rugs by having people walk on them and cars run over them. "Oh," said my Iranian friend, "that makes them more valuable. The knots become tighter and the strength greater. It is those rugs you want to buy, not the ones inside that have no wear."

People with courage are like that. They cope with the difficulties and setbacks of life and grow stronger because of them. Courageous people exemplify the saying, "When the going gets tough, the tough [courageous] get going."

A DEFINITION OF COURAGE

But what is courage? Where does it come from? Why are some people called courageous? How do they develop courage?

Aristotle and Plato understood courage as "the affirmation of one's essential being." Thomas Aquinas developed a doctrine of courage he referred to as "strength of mind, capable of conquering whatever threatens the attainment of the highest good."

A trip to the library produced a variety of books describing courageous acts, but I could find little about how courage is developed and brought into focus for one's daily activities.

Let's look at the dictionary definition again. Cour-

age is "the mental or moral strength to venture, persevere, and withstand danger, fear, or difficulty." Notice
that there is a key assumption about people with courage: they have a choice when confronted with danger,
fear, or difficulty.

The choice may be to venture into that situation of
danger, fear, or difficulty. The alternative (and the
choice of those without courage) is to remain in a safe
and protected environment.

The choice may be to persevere in a situation of
danger, fear, or difficulty. The alternative is to quit or
to flee.

The choice may be to withstand the danger, fear,
or difficulty. The alternative is to surrender.

Courage is a choice.

Why do some choose to venture instead of remain,
to persevere instead of flee, to withstand instead of surrender? The answer is that those with courage have
their eyes focused on something beyond themselves.
Courage, I have found, is a common characteristic
among those who:

- love someone dearer than themselves;
- trust in someone stronger than themselves;
- hope for something greater than themselves;
- believe in something higher than themselves.

The fascinating paradox is that only when we lose ourselves in something beyond ourselves can we hope to find such courage. By contrast, those who live only for their own needs and focus primarily on their own lives have little or no courage to venture, persevere, or withstand the danger, fear, and difficulty that will be encountered throughout life.

When Courage Is Needed

So when do those who live long and love it find the need to summon such courage?

Courage is needed in times of great loss.

The loss of a loved one, a natural disaster, a financial catastrophe—all require great courage. I remember witnessing a model of courage in a dear friend, Bill Bartel, who had a large roofing business he had spent his life building. One night on the radio I heard of a fire at Bill's warehouse. I immediately drove out to the plant and found Bill standing nearby as the fire fighters struggled to control what was obviously a total loss. I didn't know what to say as I walked over and put my hand on his shoulder. He turned to me . . . and started laughing! "Did you bring your marshmallows?" he asked.

I'm sure I had a perplexed expression on my face, for I certainly would not have felt like laughing as my life's work was going up in flames before me. "I don't know what God has in mind, but he is a lot smarter than I am," Bill said. "I'll make it. In fact, I'm looking forward to finding out what he has in store." Bill Bartel had courage.

Those with courage are able to pick themselves up and get back in the race. Those without courage find their loss to be psychologically damaging and permanent.

Courage is needed in times of great sacrifice.
Today's adults who lived through the dark years of World War II remember Winston Churchill's strong voice of courage. Who can forget his call to a nation—to a world, in fact—to muster every ounce of courage in the struggle for freedom: "Upon this battle depends the survival of Christian civilization. Upon it depends our own British life, and the long continuity of our institutions and our Empire. The whole fury and might of the enemy must very soon be turned on us. Hitler knows that he will have to break us in this island or lose the war. If we can stand up to him, all Europe may be free and the life of the world may move forward into broad, sunlit uplands. But if we fail, then the whole world, including the United States, including all that we have known and cared for, will sink into the abyss of a new Dark Age made more sinister, and perhaps more protracted, by the lights of

perverted science. Let us, therefore, brace ourselves to our duties, and so bear ourselves that, if the British Empire and its Commonwealth last for a thousand years, men will still say, 'This was their finest hour.'"[1]

Churchill actualized the words of Thomas Carlyle, who said, "Tell a man he is brave, and you help him become so."

Courage is needed in life transitions.

Turn back for a moment and study the Modified Stress Scale in chapter 4.

There's no question that people with courage are better able to handle the changes that life brings. Perhaps you can go down the list of these transitional events and think of people you know who experienced them. Who had courage and who did not? It's easy to tell, isn't it? And it's easy to see how those with courage managed the change positively and went on with their lives.

Those who lacked courage, by contrast, had a much greater struggle with change and were often permanently damaged because of it. Unfortunately, persons without courage lose more and more of themselves with each transition they face, until they can no longer face any more—and then they die.

[1] Winston Churchill, *Great Destiny* (New York: G. P. Putnam's Sons, 1962), 675.

Courage is needed to live your convictions.
We often speak of how important it is for young
people to resist peer pressure and stand up for their
convictions. But we adults are also called on occasion
to hold onto our beliefs in the face of pressure.
Courageous individuals choose to venture, persevere,
or withstand the pressure to compromise their
convictions. And they become stronger because of
their choice. Those without courage choose to remain,
to flee, or to surrender to the pressure, and they
become weaker with every such choice.

DEVELOPING COURAGE

While riding with a friend who has shown great
courage in the face of disabling cancer, I asked, "What
gave you the courage to fight back and overcome this
problem?"

He thought for a moment and replied, "A support-
ive group of friends who cared. Their caring, their regular contacts made me want to fight back."

In conversation with another friend who had
recently shown considerable courage, I asked, "Where
does courage come from?"

His answer was, "I found courage as I was able to
enlarge my frame of reference; that is, I saw something
bigger than myself." To illustrate his point, he referred
to the biblical story of Daniel and the lions' den,

observing that Daniel got his courage when he saw the bigger picture—that is, God is bigger than lions.

In my own case, as I was hospitalized with a stroke, courage to fight back came from family and friends, promises from Scripture, and the ever-growing conviction that God was not finished with me yet. There was work to be done!

I have found insight into developing courage from the classic children's story *The Wizard of Oz*. Remember the cowardly lion, supposedly the king of beasts? He set out on his journey with Dorothy to ask the wizard for the courage he thought he lacked. At one point in their journey the group was attacked by those wretched flying monkeys. The lion fought ferociously for Dorothy, Toto, the scarecrow, and the tin man—the friends he loved. Later, the wizard helped the lion realize that in his heroic act, he had indeed shown great courage—courage to fight for the ones he loved!

How to develop courage is really not something you sit down and learn. It's not a one-two-three step-by-step process. Rather, courage manifests itself as a by-product, when you:

- love someone dearer;
- trust someone stronger;
- hope for something greater;
- believe in something higher.

Pursue these worthy ends and you will discover
that when time and circumstances call for it, you are
truly courageous.

DISCUSSION QUESTIONS

1. In a group, have participants share experiences in their own lives when courage was called for.

2. What experience have you had in the last month that demanded courage?

3. The chapter lists four qualities of people who possess courage: they love someone dearer; they trust someone stronger; they hope for something greater; they believe in something higher. Do you know of anyone who illustrates one or more of these qualities?

FIGHT BACK!

6

"My name is Martha, I'm ninety-three years old, and I'm here to shake up the system."

> **Growing old is**
> **no more than a**
> **bad habit**
> **which a busy**
> **person has no**
> **time to form.**
> *Andre McIntyre*

It was July 1609, in Padua, Italy. Galileo Galilei, a mathematics professor at the University of Padua, had just learned of a remarkable invention. It was an instrument that provided an unusually clear and magnified image of distant objects. The inventor had called it a telescope.

Galileo immediately set out to learn more about the device. Upon obtaining the design, he began experimenting with how this new telescope might help him in pursuing his favorite pastime of astronomy.

The results were remarkable! He could see the moon in a way that took his breath away. And, as he improved the telescope for astronomical use, he soon discovered many more wonders of the worlds beyond his own.

But as he studied and observed the stars, he suddenly found himself contemplating an unthinkable idea. Try as he might, he could not drive it from his mind. As a result, in 1613, Galileo published "Letters on the Solar Spots."

With the publication of his letters, he single-handedly offended all the great scholars and religious leaders of his day. What Galileo had suggested was, in his day, blasphemy. He proposed that the earth was not the center of the universe and not the point around which all stars and planets revolved!

Galileo was branded by his contemporaries as a mindless fool. He was admonished by Pope Paul V to retract his heretical proposition that the sun was the center of the universe. He was threatened with prison and even death.

Imagine the pressure Galileo must have been under! Perhaps he was not entirely certain of his conclusion. Maybe he had miscalculated.

Finally, amidst growing pressure against himself and his family, Galileo capitulated, promising to obey the pope and withdraw his conclusions.

History doesn't tell us how Galileo felt or why he decided to retract his position. We do know that he continued his work in astronomy. And he apparently continued questioning the established and accepted way of thinking because seventeen years later, in 1630, he wrote "Dialogue of the Two Chief Systems of the World." In it he brilliantly expounded and defended the theory that the planets revolve around the sun, not the earth.

Again the theologians condemned his work, and selling his paper was forbidden. But this time Galileo knew he was right. This time he would fight back, regardless of what his contemporaries believed. He was summoned before the Inquisition at Rome in 1633, where he sought to defend his position. But no one would listen. Kneeling before the pope, he heard this ultimatum: Forever recant the blasphemous view that the earth moves, or be exiled for life. "It does move!" he replied as he rose from his knees.

Galileo spent the remaining years of his life in strict isolation. Only years later did astronomers realize that he had, indeed, been right. Galileo found his place in history as one of the champions of fighting back.

Senior adults who live long and love it have developed what I call the Galileo attitude. When they see what is wrong—or who is wronged—they are willing to fight back! They understand that there are times in life when someone must stand up and say, "No! That's not right!"

WHY FIGHT BACK?

Now you know and I know that there's nothing worse than an ornery, grumpy, disagreeable person. No one likes being around people like that, old or young.

So I'm not talking about a fight-back attitude that turns you into an old grouch. I'm talking about a fight-back attitude that stands up for people's rights, that insists on getting what is fairly due, that considers the rights of others as important as one's own. In fact, the fight-back attitude is often at its best when it is fighting for someone else's rights.

Here are seven reasons why I encourage you to develop a fight-back attitude:

1. Fighting back protects your rights.

I was recently in a restaurant where I ordered a bacon, lettuce, and tomato sandwich. A cluster of Thompson seedless grapes went along with the meal. When my plate arrived, I found a nice sandwich, a slice of pickle, and four scrawny little grapes on top of a patch of lettuce. They looked quite lonesome sitting there all alone.

I thought about how much I liked grapes and how I was expecting more than I had gotten. I should have asked the waitress about it, but she had gone and I was hungry. So I ate my four grapes. I grudgingly left my tip and departed with a chip on my shoulder.

I should have fought back. I had a right to more grapes, and I gave up my rights by just accepting the situation. As I think back on it, the worst that could have happened would have been the waitress explaining that they were out, or they were breaking in a new cook, or that I had received the normal helping. More than likely I would have gotten some more grapes, with a smile and an apology.

If you don't protect your rights, no one will. I think I'll go back for lunch tomorrow to the same place and see how many grapes I get. This time I'll be ready.

2. Fighting back protects the rights of others.

I personally feel much more fulfilled standing up for the rights of others than trying to get more Thompson seedless grapes for myself. You will, too.

One person who fights back is David Horowitz. I love it when he finds a fertilizer that doesn't grow fifty-pound watermelons, or gasoline that doesn't give you 25 percent more mileage, or carpet cleaner that doesn't completely remove stains left from the children's muddy boots. I will admit being impressed the time he tested a boat manufacturer's claim that their product would float even if cut in half. He actually had one of those boats chain-sawed in half right in the middle of a bay! Sure enough, both halves floated. As

David Horowitz says regularly in his crusade to protect the rights of others, "Fight back!"

While it's good to make advertising honest, there are even more significant injustices that require our fight-back energy, such as poverty, injustice, sexism, racism, and ageism, to name a few.

A modern heroine for the entire world is Mother Teresa. As a schoolteacher she was appalled to see the dead and dying in Calcutta, and she determined to do something about it. Today her mission is a world-renowned service touching many other cities and people, and she is a model of fighting for the rights of others.

Social and psychological experts agree with the timeless prescription for good health and long life: "Those who get the most give the most."

"A mere cycle of games, trips, entertainment, and handcrafts wears thin," says authority on aging Mark Bergmann. "Helping others to play games, taking others on trips, entertaining others, and making handcrafts for others, these activities give the dimension and provide the setting for the discovery of meaning."[1]

So fight back for others! There is much to be done and your help is needed. You will feel better about your own life too.

---

[1]Mark Bergmann, *Engaging the Aging in Ministry* (St. Louis: Concordia, 1981), 33.

3. Fighting back gives you hope in the future.

The poet Christina Rossetti asked, "Does the road
wind uphill all the way?" Then she answered her own
question by saying, "Yes, to the very end." She was
pointing out that we are all in a lifelong challenge that
requires vigilance, perseverance, and commitment. A
fight-back attitude gives one the confidence that
things will be better.

In the hospital after my stroke, I received a visit
from my friend Dr. Donald McGavran. At that time I
couldn't get out of bed, couldn't walk, couldn't talk
understandably. Half my body didn't work right. This
ninety-two-year old man kept assuring me that my
best days were ahead. I was so sick, I believed him!
His encouragement helped to turn up the fire in me to
fight back.

Because no two strokes are alike, I am not suggest-
ing that what happened to me can automatically be pro-
jected to others. But with the encouragement to fight
back, I determined I would leave the hospital without a
cane or a wheelchair. In my therapy sessions, I set the
goal of progressing from a wheelchair to a four-point
walking cane, to a one-point cane, to no cane at all.

Then the day arrived when I was to be dis-
charged—and I walked to the car without a cane. I did
not run or skip. But by fighting back I was able to
reach my goal.

4. Fighting back can change "the system."

We have all felt like victims of the system at one time or another. No one person really seemed to be at fault; it was just the system.

One of the memorable events in the early civil rights movement occurred one hot afternoon in the South when a group of black men and women gathered in front of a courthouse to protest a "whites only" drinking fountain on the front lawn. The police arrived with their shields, batons, and dogs and formed a line in front of the courthouse, waiting cautiously for the first signs of violence.

There was some shouting and shoving in the crowd, and it seemed as if an ugly situation was inevitable. Then out of the crowd of protesters came a slight, hunchbacked ninety-year-old black woman. She walked slowly, cane in hand, across the street toward the police line. The crowd became silent as the feeble old woman made her way toward the fountain. The white police officers slowly stepped aside as she approached.

The woman reached the fountain, put her head down, and took a drink. She then turned, passed through the police line, and slowly proceeded down the street to her home. The crowd quietly dispersed. The police returned to their station. The Whites Only sign was gone the next day.

5. Fighting back improves your self-image.

When your rights have been infringed upon, there are two possible outcomes. Both will affect your state of mind. You'll either accept the injustice and be upset with yourself and others, which will lower your self-esteem. Or you will fight back and feel better about yourself when it's over.

Fighting back gets you noticed. You are important because someone is paying attention to you. And even if you don't get all your rights, you get the respect of being heard.

When I was a young associate pastor in Portland, Oregon, I was "adopted" by an older Christian businessman in the city, George Miller. I learned a lot from that man of age and wisdom, but I particularly remember his aura of self-confidence. He seemed to assume that he would get his way. He was never improper or intimidating. It was just a way about him.

We often went out to dinner together. I remember one time he ordered a steak. When it was delivered to the table, he cut a piece, took a bite, and promptly called the waiter. He had asked for rare, and the steak was well done. He sent it back. I was embarrassed, but he simply assumed his request would be met. And it was.

Now I'm not sure that sending back your steak (or Thompson seedless grapes, for that matter) will suddenly transform you into a self-confident individual. But then again, try it and see what happens.

6. Fighting back gives you a sense of purpose.

A fight-back attitude, particularly when you fight back on behalf of others, brings with it a sense of personal contribution, mission, and value. I know some people whose entire lives have become caught up in worthy causes. A friend of mine became actively involved in M.A.D.D. (Mothers Against Drunk Driving) when her son and husband were killed by a drunk driver. Her fight-back attitude has given her a new sense of purpose in life. When significant progress is made and people are helped, our self-esteem goes up and our outlook on life improves too.

7. Fighting back gets you preferential treatment.

Most people like to be treated as special. I admit that I do. A few years ago I was taking a plane home from a seminar in Dallas. When I arrived at the airport check-in counter, I was told that the computer had inadvertently assigned my seat to someone else and that I would have to take the next flight since there were no more available seats.

I was a little upset about that since I was tired and wanted to go home. I tried to explain that I had purchased my ticket well in advance and would very much like to be on the plane. It seemed as if the woman behind the counter wasn't listening. She certainly wasn't very sympathetic with my situation. I got more and more upset, but to no avail.

Finally I told the woman I wanted to see her supervisor. It must have been that demand that got her attention. She looked more closely at her computer and then, with a pleasant smile, informed me that she had found an empty seat in first class. I would be able to fly home as planned.

Have you ever flown first class? I discovered that it was something I could easily get used to!

Can you think of examples in your own experience when you have fought back against some injustice and received a bonus beyond your normal expectations?

Fighting back means being heard—not in an obnoxious way, but with firmness, resolution, and tenacity, persevering until your goal has been realized.

THE IMPORTANCE OF FIGHTING BACK

I was recently discussing this theme with my friend Carroll Nyquist. Carroll theorized that we live in a day and age when being nice is given a higher priority than being right or speaking the truth. We all want to be well thought of and liked. Being nice is part of our culture.

I told Carroll about hearing my friend Dr. McGavran deliver a lecture in which he took strong issue with a particular view that the audience held dear. After the lecture, I said to the person in charge of the program, "I don't think I could have done that."

He responded, "Well, you're not ninety-two years old. When you're that old, you can say what you want."

Older adults do have more freedom to express themselves in honesty and forthrightness. So, as you fight back, don't hesitate to tell it like it is. You'll never have a better chance.

There are battles of many kinds still to be fought and won. You need to be on the line as part of the battle. Fighting back is something you do for yourself, but it is also something you can and should do for others.

Be an advocate. Fight back!

DISCUSSION QUESTIONS

1. In a group, ask participants to tell from their experience one incident when they fought back and won.

2. Make a list of causes and concerns where fighting back is needed today.

3. Where does fighting back cross the line into selfishness?

"Did You Hear the One About....?"

7

A cheerful
***
heart is good
***
medicine.
***
Solomon

*F*or centuries, laughter and positive emotions have been known to contribute to people's health, healing, and happiness. Scripture records that "a cheerful heart is good medicine."[1] So senior adults—or anyone else who desires to live long and love it—will want to keep a twinkle in their eye and a merry heart.

To be able to laugh at oneself, at the foolishness of the world, at problems—to laugh when things aren't funny—that is a secret of those who enjoy a long and happy life. There is healing in humor.

While I was in physical therapy recovering from my stroke, I determined to build relationships through

[1]Proverbs 17:22, New International Version.

humor. Since doctors, nurses, and therapists hear so many complaints and negativisms, I tried beginning each therapy session by sharing a joke or humorous story. It turned out that even some of my dumbest little quips made their way around the hospital.

My joke one day was the one about the young snake who came to its mother and asked, "Mother, are we poisonous?"

"Yes," replied his mother, "very, very poisonous. Why do you ask?"

The little snake answered, "Because I just bit my tongue!"

When a different therapist a few days later asked me if I had heard about the young snake, I realized many people had enjoyed my humor therapy.

HUMOR AS THERAPY

When Norman Cousins, author of twenty books, was confronted with the diagnosis of a terminal illness, he began fighting back by using both medicine and humor. He looked at all the old Three Stooges movies, reruns of "Candid Camera," and other humorous videos he could find. He found joke books and combed them for the funniest stories. After a time, his prognosis changed and he recovered. He credited his healing, in large part, to the power of the mind over the body. Following his recovery, Cousins spent many years as a counselor to physicians on the value of positive mental attitudes in the healing process.

How does laughter help people get well? Humor is not a cure-all. But when used with appropriate medication prescribed by a physician, humor brings a positive and healing dimension. Remember, "A cheerful heart is good medicine."

Our emotions produce measurable physical changes—some positive, some negative. Anger increases the heart rate. Add fear to anger and the heart rate increases even more. Worry triggers gastrointestinal juices that contribute to ulcers.

In contrast, happiness and other positive emotions produce positive effects in the body. Many scientists believe that hearty laughter helps the human brain produce endorphins and enkephalins. These morphine-like molecules serve as painkillers and help to release the full range of positive emotions.

WHAT DOES AN ENDORPHIN LOOK LIKE?

As a layman thinking about medical science, I try to visualize what endorphins look like. Since I have never seen a picture of them, my imagination gives them fanciful forms. At one time I see them as something like a tadpole. When I give a hearty laugh, their tails massage my organs.

At other times I envision them with long whiskers

ourselves? Or is the tonic of laughter randomly bestowed on a select few who always seem to delight in seeing the lighter side of life?

First, it is important to realize that becoming a humorist is not the same as developing a sense of humor. "Many great humorists have little or no sense of humor," says Carolyn Wells, author of *The World's Best Humor*. "Such was the case with Dickens, Carlyle, and many other renowned wits. The humorist without a sense of humor is a bore. The person with a sense of humor is a joy to know and to be with."

While you or I may never become a great humorist, we can all develop and cultivate our sense of humor. I personally used to believe that a sense of humor, and some people's unusual ability to see the funny side of life, was a quality they had been born with and I had not. I have come to realize, however, that such is not the case.

Cultivating a sense of humor is actually much like developing a taste for music or the fine arts. While a particular taste or sense may be more natural in some people than others, we can all broaden our enjoyment of good humor.

Aristotle thought a great deal about humor and sought after it. He defined humor as "that which is incongruous—out of its proper place and time, yet without danger or pain."

The great Roman orator Cicero suggested that "the most enjoyable kind of humor is when we expect to hear one thing and hear another."[3] Cicero might well have enjoyed this true story of an early American preacher:

The minister, on Temperance Sunday, to offer indisputable proof of the evil effects of liquor, created an elaborate demonstration with a worm. He first dropped the worm into a glass of clear water where it wiggled about with apparent delight. Then he removed it and dropped it into a glass of whiskey, where it died instantly. "Now what does this prove?" the preacher asked, beaming with satisfaction. A red-eyed brother from the rear rose up and answered: "If you drink plenty of whiskey, you'll never have worms!"[4]

Here are four suggestions on how to begin cultivating your sense of humor.

Step 1: Expose yourself to good humor.

There are plenty of good humorous books that make for enjoyable reading in your evening hours. Authors

---

[3]The quotations from Carolyn Wells, Aristotle, and Cicero are from *The World's Best Humor* (New York: Albert Boni Publishers, 1923), 18, 12, 15.   [4]Ross Phares, *Bible in Pocket, Gun in Hand* (Lincoln, Nebr.: University Press, 1964), 63.

like Erma Bombeck, Bill Cosby, Art Buchwald, and Andy Rooney have created masterpieces of good humor. You don't even need to buy the books. Just go to your local library and check them out for a few weeks. If you hear of a famous comedian coming to your area, buy some tickets and go enjoy a good laugh.

Step 2: Do something silly.

We tend to lose one of the wonderful joys of childhood as we move into the self-conscious years of adolescence, and many people don't ever get it back. It's the fun of being silly.

A few months ago my daughter and her family came from Alaska to visit for a few days. It so happened that on one night of their stay there was to be a full lunar eclipse. I don't recall now how the idea first came up, but someone suggested we should have a "moon party."

Now, no one in either of our families had any experience at moon parties, so we all began offering our suggestions. It turned out to be quite a memorable event.

As the party began, each of us received a special "moon hat" that, unless you knew better, looked curiously like those newspaper pirate hats we used to make when we were kids. We then played a round of "moon charades," where each person had to act out the name of a planet. Following that, we adjourned to the kitchen for some "moon juice" (not moonshine, mind you).

After a few more moon games we all went out onto the front driveway to watch the eclipse. Then, as we had practiced earlier, just at the moment the earth's shadow moved completely in front of the moon, we all crossed our arms in front of us, waved them up and down, and let out the most unearthly "moon howl" you have ever heard. One of our neighbors came outside to see who was hurt! But we all had a wonderful time. (Maybe it is true what they say about the effect of the full moon on people's behavior!)

Your assignment for this step is to go do something silly. It's more fun when you do it with other people, rather than hidden behind a locked door. But if it helps, you can try a few silly things there first. Don't worry about your reputation. If anything, it will improve!

Step 3: Laugh out loud, whether you feel like it or not.

Hearing yourself laugh actually causes you to laugh even more. Try it right now. Just start laughing out loud. Then listen to yourself. Pretty soon you will be laughing at your own laughing! If you think that's funny, try getting three or four of your friends together and do the same thing. Tell the group that on the count of three you are all going to start laughing. Before you know it, you'll be rolling in the aisles.

I remember a game we used to play when I was growing up. Everyone in our family would lie on the floor, each with his or her head on someone else's stomach. Then one person would begin laughing. The chain reaction of heads bouncing on laughing stomachs would spread, and soon our entire family would be howling hysterically. As we thought about how silly we must all look, we found ourselves laughing even harder.

The next time you hear or see something funny, laugh out loud. Don't just smile or chuckle. Laugh! You'll find that it is both therapeutic and contagious. And the time after that, you'll find you won't have to work as hard to get the laugh out.

Step 4: Tell one funny story each day for the next two weeks.

You may have to go down to the library if you run out of ammunition. That's okay. But see if you can get one person to laugh aloud each day at something humorous you share. If you're telling a joke, practice it beforehand to get the greatest impact. And be sure, when you finish the punch line, to enjoy it and laugh at the joke yourself. Pretend it is the first time you've heard it.

Speaking of good stories, I heard one the other day that was placed in the early days of this world's history. God had just created Adam and Eve. Adam began to question his Maker: "God, when you made Eve, why did you give her such nice hair and smooth skin?"

"So you would like her," God responded.

"But God, you made her body different from mine. She has bumps and bulges in places that are quite different from mine. Why did you make her like that, God?"

Again God replied, "So you would like her, Adam."

A third time Adam spoke to God: "But God, there is one thing. She is quite stupid. In fact, she is downright dumb! Why did you make her like that?"

Patiently God responded, "So she would like you, Adam."

Another creation story—After God had made Adam, he looked at what he had done, shook his head and said, "I can do better than that!" So he created Eve.

DR. SEUSS
As parents, most of us have read to our children the imaginative stories of Theodor Seuss Geisel, better known as Dr. Seuss. *The Grinch That Stole Christmas, The Cat in the Hat, Yertle the Turtle,* and others have brought him honors from seven universities, a Pulitzer prize, and Emmy and Peabody awards.

What a pleasant surprise it was to learn that Dr.
Seuss, at age eighty-two, had published a book entitled *You're Only Old Once!* for his millions of fans now
turned seniors. On the back cover is the question, "Is
this a children's book?" The answer: "Well . . . not
immediately. You buy a copy for your child now and
you give it to him on his 70th birthday." The book is a
wonderful example of Dr. Seuss's usual wit and delightful humor. If laughter is the best medicine, then *You're
Only Old Once!* is a wonderful new defense against
aging.[5]

Speaking of children, I heard the other day of a
ninety-eight-year-old husband and his ninety-four-
year-old wife who visited their attorney to seek a
divorce. "Why, after all these years, would you now
decide to get a divorce?" the lawyer asked.

"Oh, that's easy," replied the husband. "We wanted
to wait until the children died."

If you are faced with the option of laughing or crying, choose laughter and, in time, there may be no reason for tears.

By the way, did you know there are three ways you
can tell if you're getting old? The first is, you start forgetting things.

Let's see . . . what were the other two?

---

[5]Dr. Seuss, *You're Only Old Once!* (New York: Random House, 1986).

"WHERE'S GRANDMA?"

Speaking about forgetting, did you hear about the grandfather and grandmother who planned a trip to visit their grandchildren? Driving down the road, the grandfather had that strange feeling that he had forgotten something. He took out his wallet and checked for money and his driver's license. All was in order.

Driving farther, he was still bothered by the same feeling. He pulled the car to the side of the road, got out, looked in the trunk, and checked the luggage. Nothing seemed to be missing, so he drove on.

When the car pulled into the driveway, his little grandson came running out of the house and exclaimed, "Hi, Grandpa! Where's Grandma?"

I recently told that story to a friend who said, "Something just like that actually happened in my family." Her father and mother were driving to visit one of their children when they pulled into a service station for gas. Her mother went to use the restroom while her father paid for the gas—and proceeded on the trip with his wife still in the restroom! The father didn't realize his wife's absence until she didn't answer his question about lodging for the night!

All of this seemed humorous—until it happened to me. Having made arrangements for my wife to pick me up in the car after a one-mile walk, I expected to see her at the appointed time. I waited and waited. No sign of her. Thirty minutes later I was still waiting, knowing she had forgotten. Forty-five minutes later, I looked up and there she came. She was most apologetic. Indeed, she had forgotten her husband of forty-three years. My only remark was, "Hi, Grandma! Where's Grandpa?"

"A cheerful heart is good medicine." Have a good laugh today, and then share it with someone else.

DISCUSSION QUESTIONS

1. In your group or with your friends, share the best humorous story you know.

2. List ways that a merry heart and laughter can be developed and shared.

3. Can you recall experiences that seemed anything but funny at the time but have their funny side now as you look back at them?

LEARNING TO LOVE

8

"You've been a good friend, Bud, and I love you...
pardon the expression."

> **To each and**
> **every one of**
> **us, love gives**
> **the promise**
> **of working**
> **miracles**
> **if we will.**
>
> *Lydia Child*

*I*ntimate relationships make a profound difference in the quality of life at any age," says Ken Dychtwald in *Age Wave*. "Yet, in later years of life, the making and keeping of relationships can become more difficult."[1]

Senior adults who are living long and loving it have developed ways to focus outside their own problems and concerns. They are not wrapped up in their own worlds but have learned the importance and value of getting out of themselves.

One of the best ways of doing this is by learning to love!

[1]Dychtwald and Flower, *Age Wave*, 209.

Love is the great life-giver for senior adults who experience it—and the great void for those living without it.

SENIORS KNOW THE MOST ABOUT LOVING

Based on a research study we conducted several years ago and recently reevaluated in light of the age variable, senior adults seem to be, of all age groups, most able to give and receive love. Here are a few fascinating observations.

Among those who participate in their church Bible classes, 94 percent of adults over the age of sixty-four indicated they experience a high degree of love and caring. By contrast, only 65 percent of young adults reported the same feeling of love and caring in their classes. Among adults between the ages of twenty-one and sixty-five, 78 percent expressed that feeling.

Respondents were asked: "On a scale of 1–10 (with 10 as 'easiest'), how easy is it to say 'I love you' to the following persons?" The following graph shows the results.

Notice how it becomes easier for us to say "I love you" the older we grow. With only a few exceptions, there is an increase at every age level in every category. Young people, for example, find it extremely difficult to say "I love you" to others. In fact, it is easier for people over sixty-five years to say "I love you" to other friends (at the bottom of their list) than it is for people under twenty to say those same words to their own family members.

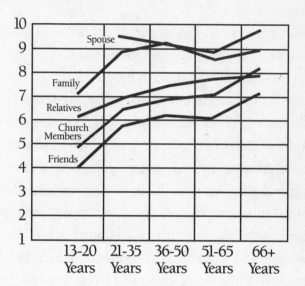

THE POWER OF LOVE

The power of love may be mysterious, but it has never been a secret. History and literature are full of famous quotations about love. Victor Hugo said that "the great happiness of life is the conviction that we are loved . . . loved for ourselves, or rather, loved in spite of ourselves."

Martin Luther once commented that "faith, like light, must always be simple and unbending; while love, like warmth, should beam forth on every side and bend to every necessity of our brethren."

William Penn said that "love is the hardest lesson in Christianity; but for that reason, it should be most our care to learn it."[2]

Today there are indications that love is necessary for survival. One study found that people who live alone and have few or no close friends have a mortality rate equal to that of two-pack-a-day cigarette smokers.[3]

It has been proven that people without loving support in time of sickness take longer to recover. In serious cases, patients without the caring support of friends and family die sooner than those who know their lives have value to others. A research physician at Johns Hopkins University calls loneliness the number one killer. "Some other illness goes on the death certificate," he maintains, "but the prime cause was loneliness."[4]

We need others. We can't make it entirely on our own. The human being has the longest dependency period of any living organism. We begin life with a love need, and we never completely outgrow it.

A HUNGER FOR LOVE

Yet, in spite of our crying need for it, many find love difficult to express. In an enlightening research study,

---

[2]Hugo, Luther, and Penn are quoted in Win Arn & Charles Arn, *Who Cares about Love?* (Monrovia, Calif.: Church Growth Press, 1986), 170, 185, 41. [3]Sheila Sobel Maramarco, "Friendship: The Tie That Binds You in Good Health," *PSA Magazine* (January 1983): 32-34. [4]Fred Smith, "The Gift of Greeting," *Christianity Today* (13 December 1985): 70.

a group of people were asked to approach those whom they loved and verbally express their love. Almost all participants later reported being tongue-tied, ill at ease, awkward, and embarrassed. In discussing their experiences, they agreed that "it was strange, indeed, that so many found it threatening to communicate love." The researcher observed that "it became obvious why we hear the voice of love so seldom; and when it is heard, it is spoken so softly, so shyly . . . even though we have learned that unexpressed love is the greatest cause of our sorrow and regret."[5]

"I have seen the starving in the world," said Mother Teresa following a visit to the United States, "but in your country I have seen an even greater hunger, and that is the hunger to be loved. No place in all my travels have I seen such loneliness as I have seen in the poverty of affluence in America."[6]

WHAT IS LOVE?
Let me briefly suggest a definition of love that I have found helpful and then share seven simple, yet powerful, steps to bring out the natural lover in you.

The definition: *Love is intentionally doing something caring for another person, regardless of the cost or consequence to oneself.*

[5]Leo F. Buscaglia, *Loving Each Other* (Thorofare, N.J.: Slack, 1984), 54. [6]*Guideposts* (January 1988): 85.

Consider the key words and phrases:

Intentionally—Love does not happen by accident, but because it is planned and premeditated. Love determines to act in a particular way.

Doing something—Love is action. If it is not seen or observed or experienced on a regular basis, there is cause to doubt whether it is really love. The apostle John says, "Let us stop just *saying* we love people; let us *really* love them, and *show it* by our actions."[7]

Caring—The ultimate act of caring is giving one's own life to protect the object of one's love. The Scriptures illustrate this truth: "This is how we know what love is: Jesus Christ laid down his life for us. And we ought to lay down our lives for our brothers."[8]

For another person—Love is always focused on people. Love does not exist in a vacuum. Self-interest is not what motivates loving action. The well-being and interest of the person who is loved motivates action.

Regardless of the cost or consequence to oneself— True love puts others ahead of oneself. It does not say, "I love you if it doesn't cost anything, or if it's convenient, or if I don't hurt myself in the process." Can you imagine God putting those conditions on his love for us? Again, the Scriptures, as God's love story

[7] 1 John 3:18, *The Living Bible.*   [8] 1 John 3:16, New International Version.

to us, say, "Therefore be imitators of God, as beloved children. And walk in love, as Christ loved us and gave himself up for us, a fragrant offering and sacrifice to God."[9]

So, the love we are describing is not passion, it is compassion; not selfish, but selfless; not inward-focused, but outward-focused.

SEVEN STEPS TO LOVING

Can we learn to love, or to love better? Can we initiate and nurture loving relationships? The answer is an absolute *yes!* Here are seven steps to help you become a better lover. Try them. They work!

Step 1: Identify those who need your love.

The first step in experiencing the joy of love is to identify two or three people to practice on. Select them from the following categories:

Family. Father, mother, spouse, children, in-laws, grandparents, nephews, aunts—anyone related to you biologically or through marriage.

Friends. Those whose company you enjoy—people you'd invite to dinner or take to a concert. Ones with whom you share common interests.

Acquaintances. People you know casually as a

---

[9] Ephesians 5:1-2, Revised Standard Version.

neighbor, colleague, or fellow member in a church, club, or activity.

The needy. Someone you know with a physical, emotional, or personal need. The Bible makes the pointed comment, "If any one has the world's goods and sees his brother in need, yet closes his heart against him, how does God's love abide in him?"[10]

Enemies. Jesus was right: "If you love only those who love you, what good is that? Even scoundrels do that much."[11]

Step 2: Act first.

So often we wait for the other person to act. Will she smile? Will he speak first? Will they invite us over?

Don't wait for the other person. Always act first! And act not just once, but again and again—whatever is necessary to make the relationship come alive. Make a life-style of taking the initiative and acting first.

Step 3: Communicate.

Research shows that most Americans believe the key ingredient in a loving relationship is communication.[12] They're probably right. As communication grows, love grows.

---

[10] John 3:17, Revised Standard Version. [11] Matthew 5:46, *The Living Bible*. When he said, "Love your enemies," he defined enemies as those who speak ill of you, hate you, mistreat you, or harass you. (Try selecting one person to practice on from this group and watch what happens. It's great!) [12] Buscaglia, *Loving*, 36.

Most communication occurs at one of the following four levels. Ask yourself, "At which level do I communicate with the persons identified in Step 1?"

- Exchange of *clichés*. "Hi! How are you?" "Fine, how are you?" "Have a nice day!"
- Exchange of *information*. "Did you hear about the Dodger pitcher who was traded yesterday?" "It's supposed to rain tomorrow."
- Exchange of *attitudes*. "I really think this issue is important for our community." "I surely would like to know how to grow beautiful roses."
- Exchange of *feelings*. "I was really frightened last night." "I'm sorry you feel that way."

Try communicating one level deeper in the coming week with the two or three persons you identified. If your conversation is mostly limited to clichés, try talking about the news or the weather. If you talk about ideas, stretch yourself and share some feelings. Admit a fear or hurt, frustration, or disappointment. And share your joys!

Step 4: Empathize.
Empathy is identification with, or vicariously experiencing, the thoughts, feelings, or attitudes of another person. In a sense, you become that person.

You see the world through the other person's eyes. You experience what she experiences. You feel what he feels.

A news service recently carried a moving example of loving empathy. It was about a man with cancer and his friends and family who said, "We love you."

Manuel Garcia dreaded shaving his head to get rid of the patches of hair left by chemotherapy. He was afraid he would feel very self-conscious. He thought everyone would stare at him.

He didn't need to worry.

Before Garcia was released from the Milwaukee Medical Complex after treatment, his friend and three relatives came into his room with bald heads.

"I woke up and just started laughing," said Garcia. "Then they told me, 'We're here so you won't be alone.'"

When he arrived home, his house and neighborhood were teeming with bald heads— all in the name of love for Manuel Garcia in his fight against cancer.

"My oldest boy had beautiful hair," said Garcia of his son who had his head shaved. "Last night he said, 'Daddy, I did it because I love you.'"

"I cut my hair because I've known him for 15 years and I love him like a father," said Dale Wetzel, 26. "It helped me to understand how he felt; it made me feel good inside."

When Garcia had been diagnosed as having cancer, he was extremely depressed. "But I'm ready for anything now," he says. "I feel 100% better."[13]

When you begin to empathize, to see the world from the other person's perspective, you are beginning to love.

Step 5: Identify a love opportunity.

As you begin to see the world from the perspective of the people you are learning to love, you will identify *their* needs and *your* opportunities. A love opportunity may be meeting physical, emotional, relational, or spiritual needs. Everyone has needs. Our task is to identify what those needs are. Then we can take the next step.

Step 6: Respond with a caring gift.

A good gift is a wonderful expression of love and will say much more than words. Learning to be a good

[13]"Hair is Where the Heart Is," *Pasadena Star News* (20 July 1985): D-5.

gift-giver is an important part of learning to love.

A good gift has four characteristics.

It is *meaningful*—based on the need of the person receiving it.

It is *sacrificial*—otherwise it is just a convenience.

It is *unexpected*—rather than predictable due to protocol or expectation.

It is *motivated by love*—unconditionally, with no expectation of return.

The best gifts may not be purchased at the local shopping mall. You can give the gift of forgiveness to a person with whom you've argued. You can give the gift of appreciation to a person who feels neglected. You can give the gift of support to a person who is alone and uncertain.

Step 7: Share yourself.

Sharing your most treasured possession is hard to do because it's all you have—it's you. The ultimate step of love is to give yourself.

Sharing yourself means loving another person as yourself. The Bible says, "So we also ought to lay down our lives for our Christian brothers." "Love your neighbor as yourself" has been called the great commandment for all to follow.[15]

---

[14]1 John 3:16, *The Living Bible*   [15]Mark 12:33, New International Version.

On the editorial page of a local newspaper a few years ago, I read a moving illustration of this ultimate step of love:

Just about everyone knows the Jim Brady story—the man who, only two months after becoming White House press secretary, was shot in the head during the attempted assassination of President Reagan; and how he has fought his way back from brain surgery and the crippling, enduring damage from the stray bullet.

Not many people know, however, about the ceaseless, selfless, single-minded devoted love of Bob Dahlgren . . . a man who loved Brady like himself.

A few months ago, Bob Dahlgren died in his sleep, at 52 years of age. It didn't even make the morning news. But during the long months following the shooting, it was Dahlgren who took the vigil with Brady's wife, Sarah, through the long series of brain operations.

It was Dahlgren and his wife, Suzie, who took Brady's young son Scott into their home through the early days of the ordeal.

It was Dahlgren who arranged the happy

hours with Brady's friends by his hospital bedside.

As Brady recovered and returned to a semi-normal life, it was Dahlgren, always Dahlgren, who scouted out the advance arrangements, who helped load and unload his friend from the specially equipped van in which Brady did most of his traveling.

It was Dahlgren who helped Sarah field the questions about Brady's health and spent endless hours keeping friends posted on his condition. It was Dahlgren who helped organize a foundation to assure financial support for the family.

For more than four and a half years after Brady was shot, Bob Dahlgren devoted virtually all his time to the man he loved. And he did so with little recognition and no hint of seeing anything in return. Never, ever did Dahlgren complain. Never did he hesitate when needed. Never did he stop looking for the needs or the response of love.

As Dr. Arthur Kobrine, the surgeon who lived through Brady's long ordeal with him, once said, "Everyone should have a friend like Bob Dahlgren."[16]

[16]Raymond Coffey, "He Was Jim Brady's Best Friend," *Pasadena Star News* (3 November 1985): A-5.

Learning the steps—and the benefits—of love is one of the most exciting and rewarding things a person can do in life. And the best part is that it's an endeavor you can keep enjoying. There's always more to learn about love, more people who are in need of love, and more joy to receive through love.

We can learn to love! Senior adults who live long and love it have discovered that when love is given, it comes back many times over.

SEEING LOVE OPPORTUNITIES

To conclude this chapter I would like to share with you a true story. Yet it is also a parable—a parable about how we can easily become oblivious to the wonderful possibilities available to us. The story illustrates how you and I can have the rich rewards of love right now through the persons around us, if we will take the time to learn and pursue its wealth.

The story is about a farmer who lived in the mountains of Africa. This farmer owned a very large farm with orchards, grain fields, and gardens. He was a contented, wealthy man—contented because he was wealthy, and wealthy because he was contented!

One day a visitor came to his farm and described the fortunes being made by people discovering diamond mines. He described in vivid detail the beautiful stones looking like drops of congealed sunlight. He claimed that a handful of diamonds would purchase all the desires of the heart, placing his children on thrones around the world through the influence of his great wealth.

That night the farmer went to bed a poor man, although he had not lost a thing. He was poor because he was discontented, and discontented because he feared he was poor. As the farmer lay on his bed thinking of wealth, he said aloud: "I want a mine of diamonds."

All night he lay awake thinking about diamonds. Early in the morning he sought out the stranger for directions to where these gleaming gems might be found. He was told that they were found in white sands between high mountains.

"I will go!" said the farmer. So he sold his farm, left his family with a neighbor, and went away in search of diamonds. He searched through mountains and valleys, through deserts and plains. At last, when his money was spent and he was in rags, wretched and ruined, he stood on a bridge with swirling water below. That poor, afflicted, suffering man could not resist the awful temptation to cast himself into the water, where he sank beneath the dark surface, never to rise in this life again.

Some time later, the man who purchased the farm noticed a curious flash of light on the bank of a stream running through the farm. He reached in and pulled out a black stone having an eye of light that reflected the colors of the rainbow. He took the curious pebble into the house, left it on the mantel, and forgot all about it.

Some days later the same stranger returned. When he saw that flash of light from the mantel, he rushed up to it and said, "Here is a diamond! Here is a diamond!"

"No, no," said the owner, "this is not a diamond. It is just a stone I found in my stream."

"It is a diamond," insisted the stranger.

Together they returned to the stream and stirred up the white sands with their fingers. There they found other diamonds, more beautiful and more valuable than the first. Thus was discovered the diamond mine of Golconda, the most magnificent diamond mine in all the history of humankind.

The first farmer had owned literally acres of diamonds. For every acre—yes, every shovelful of that old farm—contained the gleaming gems. Yet he had sold them for practically nothing, for money to look for diamonds elsewhere. Had he only taken the time and expended the effort to know what diamonds look like in their rough state, and had he first explored the land he owned, he would have had the riches he sought right under his own feet![17]

[17]Quoted in Charles Arn, *Growth: A New Vision for the Sunday School* (Pasadena: Church Growth Press, 1980), 145-47.

What a wonderful story about the obvious fact that each of us, at this moment, is standing on our own "acres of diamonds" if we but have the wisdom, the vision, and the determination to explore our possibilities right where we are.

All around you are love opportunities. They are people who represent to you a wealth of meaningful, loving relationships. While you can walk on top of them and around them, oblivious to the possibilities they hold, you can also see them from a new perspective. You can see the hidden possibilities in each person, possibilities which love can bring to the surface. And these love opportunities hold riches beyond your greatest imagination.

Look down at your feet. Brush away the sand. There! Did you see it? That flash of brilliant light? You are standing on acres of diamonds, and they are yours for the taking. Learn to love!

DISCUSSION QUESTIONS

1. Identify two or three people in your world who are possible targets for love.

2. Select one person on your list and determine several appropriate ways of expressing love.

3. Set specific dates by which you will have taken the steps listed in number 2 above.

STRETCHING YOUR LIMITS

9

"I try to make sure my ignorance and my hairline recede at roughly the same rate."

> Ah, but a man's
> reach should
> exceed his
> grasp,
> Or what's a
> heaven for?
>
> *Robert Browning*

*O*liver Wendell Holmes, Supreme Court justice, was asked why he had taken up the study of Greek at the age of ninety-four. Holmes replied, "Why, my good sir, it's now or never!"

That's the spirit of *stretching your limits*, which I encourage each reader of this book to consider and act upon. Maybe we won't all study Greek. But exploring and even extending the limits of one's own ability is a secret of those who live long and love it.

Claude Pepper, who for years in the U.S. Congress championed the rights of senior adults, echoed this theme. At age eighty-six Pepper said, "The later years need not be a time of retreat. We can't control aging since it goes on daily, but we can control our attitude toward it. We can refuse to resign ourselves to a diminished role in life just because another candle has been added to the birthday cake. I am convinced that a positive attitude is the secret of youth. The point I want to make is this: you adapt, and you keep going to the limits of your ability."[1]

STRETCH YOUR LIMITS . . . PHYSICALLY

Sister Mary Martin Weaver took up athletics at the age of fifty-five. In the last ten years she has won forty-four medals. A Roman Catholic nun, Sister Mary participates in a variety of athletic events, including the five-thousand-meter race walk, snowshoe racing, speed and figure skating, basketball free throws, shotput, and ice hockey. The four-foot-eleven-inch Sister Mary is a regular participant at the Rocky Mountain Senior Games in the U.S. National Senior Olympics. She competes in her black and white habit of the Order of St. Dominic. As her main vocation, Sister Mary is a registered nurse in a nursing home.

How and why does she find time for athletics? Sister Mary says, "Working in a nursing home is awfully hard mentally, physically, and spiritually. If you're not careful, you get burned out. That's why more people

[1]Quo. :d in Joe E. Barnett, *Live It Up!* (Cleveland, Tenn.: Pathway Publishing, 1988), 21.

should get into athletics. It makes your blood pump, your lungs work, your tensions disappear; and, if that's not enough, it's fun! What people my age sometimes forget is that there is so much more to life than sitting in a chair and getting old! Who on earth wants that?

"People have gotten flabby and I don't mean just physically," Sister Mary continues. "Anything that's too much, people just don't want to do. The thing is, there are no rewards unless you try. Age should never be a barrier to full participation in life. A good diet is important; exercise is important; but what's most important is to enjoy life to its fullest, to do things for others, and never, ever be afraid to stretch your limits!"[2]

STRETCH YOUR LIMITS . . . MENTALLY

Tom and Holly Hollis of Wasilla, Alaska, are further examples of senior adults who are stretching their limits. Holly, the oldest child of a large Dutch immigrant family, long ago dreamed of becoming a teacher. But, as was common in those days, she had to quit high school and help with the family's living. Not until her own children were grown was she able to reach one of her personal goals.

[2]Peter Swet, "Stretch Your Limits," *Parade* (15 July 1990): 10.

Never a quitter, Holly enrolled in classes at the local community college and earned her two-year degree. "One of the pleasures of attending school at my age," says Holly, "is that you have lived through most of the history the class is studying. And by golly, if the book was wrong about the way things happened, I stood up and told them so."

Holly discovered that the brain becomes lazy over the years. It took concentration to excel in her studies. But as a pleasant surprise, Holly found that the extra mental energy she exerted carried over into other areas of her life. Never before had she felt as sharp-witted and interested in a wide variety of topics. Enjoying the sense of accomplishment she received in continuing her education, Holly decided to finish her bachelor's degree. She graduated with honors!

Holly's husband, Tom, an electronics engineer, had always hoped to continue his education as well. But he had found long ago that going to school and supporting a family was impossible. Several times he tried to arrange for a paid study leave, but it never worked out. In retirement, Tom enjoyed watching Holly realize her educational dreams. After Holly's graduation, Tom asked her, "Well, what do you want to do now?" Her immediate answer: "Get a master's degree."

By this time Tom had spent enough nights alone or watching Holly study. He decided that his opportunity to get more education had also come. So together they commuted forty miles each way to Alaska Pacific University, often in severe weather conditions.

Holly and Tom found themselves the only senior citizen couple attending the university. "We kept each other going," says Tom. "We found we could share our strengths with the other, and we helped each other when the going got tough. We knew we would enjoy the subject matter, but one of the unexpected pleasures was our association with professors and the more mature students we found at the graduate level."

On May 5, 1990, Tom and Holly Hollis received their master's degrees. As the dean called their names and they walked across the stage, the entire auditorium erupted in cheers and applause. It had been a long road for the little girl from Holland who had to quit school. But she had stretched her limits and gone for it.

Holly and Tom realized lifelong goals, and if that wasn't enough, they had fun along the way.

MY OWN STRETCHING PLAN

I try to practice what I preach. So at age sixty-eight, I'm going back to school. I've decided to go to the University of Southern California School of Gerontology, one of the two schools in the nation that give a doctorate in this field.

I can think of many reasons why I shouldn't go back to school. It's expensive—wow!—far more so than when I attended college and seminary years ago. It takes time, and I'm already too busy to get done everything I'd like. Since my stroke, I also have trouble with my vision. Reading is much more difficult than before.

Why, then, do I want to go back to school? I want to be challenged intellectually. Brain cells come to life as one uses them. "Use it or lose it" applies not only to physical health but to mental ability as well.

Another reason is that I am a senior adult myself. I'd like to read and discuss what that's all about with the best minds in the field.

Finally, I expect to share my new knowledge through lectures, books, and videos, so I want my information to be accurate, fresh, and new.

And, as Oliver Wendell Holmes said, "Why, my good sir, it's now or never!" I'll see you in class.

STRETCH YOUR LIMITS . . . SPIRITUALLY

Dr. Ted Engstrom, a long-time friend who for years was president of World Vision, tells the story of Denny and Jeanne Grindall from Seattle, Washington.

Denny and Jeanne wrestled for some time with the issue of what the Lord wanted them to do in their retirement years. They are warm, committed Christians, and the love of Christ shines through their entire being; but they both admit, "We are just ordinary people . . . very ordinary."

The Grindalls decided to take a journey, a simple tourist trip, for several months, leaving their successful florist business in Seattle. While they were in Kenya, East Africa, they were taken by missionary friends to the nomadic Masai people. They found these people living a primitive life; their death rate extremely high and life expectancy low. The Grindalls found chickens, pigs, and other animals living with humans in the little mud huts. Together, Denny and Jeanne determined they would go back to live among these fascinating people and work together with them in programs of community development.

The Grindalls decided to assist the Masai in learning how to obtain vitally needed water, build pigpens, and develop sanitation facilities. They wanted to share their knowledge in horticulture and give guidance from their own experience. Today, six months out of every year, this post-middle age couple lives among the Masai and are beautifully accepted by these formerly nomadic people. The once unsanitary huts have been cleaned out. The quality of health has improved greatly, and people are living longer. Children are no longer suffering from malnutrition, and the lives of whole communities have been tremendously improved through the loving, caring concern of these loving Christians from the Pacific Northwest.[3]

GETTING STARTED

How do you go about stretching your limits and discovering new frontiers of growth? Here are five simple steps to help you get started:

First, determine if you really want to go for it. If you don't, I suggest you stop here and go on to the next chapter. But if you do want to continue to grow, which is really what stretching your limits is all about, take the next step.

Second, select one of the three areas listed in this chapter—physical, mental, or spiritual—in which to stretch your limits.

Third, find a "stretching partner." This is a person who also wants to grow and stretch his or her limits in this area.

Fourth, discuss with this person how to go about stretching your limits. Set some specific one-month, three-month, and six-month goals.

[3]Ted Engstrom and Robert Larson, *Seizing the Torch* (Ventura, Calif.: Regal Press, 1979), 126.

Fifth, chart your progress. Keep a diary of where you are when you start, and then update it weekly.

In no time at all, you'll find you have grown measurably—and immeasurably! And you'll discover what Sister Mary Martin Weaver, the nun who snowshoes, speed skates, throws the shotput, and stars in ice hockey, has also discovered. Stretching yourself "makes your blood pump, your lungs work, your tensions disappear; and, if that's not enough, it's fun! What people my age sometimes forget is that there is so much more to life than sitting in a chair and getting old!"

DISCUSSION QUESTIONS

Share with members of your group or with friends how you would like to stretch your limits physically, mentally, and spiritually.

CHANGING GARMENTS... & MOVING ON

10

"What's your biblical basis for believing that 'heaven will be a lot like Sandusky, Ohio, in 1937'?"

The best
is yet
to be.
Robert Browning

*S*enior adults who live long and love it have come to terms with the exit of life—death. They realize that death is everyone's lot and that it can come expectedly or unexpectedly. Death doesn't allow denial or indecision, but these senior adults have learned that if one chooses to deal with it openly and honestly, death need not have the last word.

Views of death vary tremendously. Some people hold to what Robert Fulghum calls the kindergarten approach—"gold fish, hamsters, and white mice, and even the little seeds in the styrofoam cup . . . they all die. So do we."[1]

---

[1]Stephan Kanfer, "Sermons from Rev. Feelgood," *Time* (2 July 1990):58.

Others hold to Shakespeare's view in *Julius Caesar*—that "Imperial Caesar, dead and turned to clay, has no exclusive rights over that deep universal embrace which will receive us all."

Or, as in Bryant's "Thanatopsis," we have no need to go "like the quarry-slave at night, scourged to his dungeon," but can approach death "like one who wraps the drapery of his couch about him and lies down to pleasant dreams."

Tertullian, an early Christian leader, likened death to sleep, and resurrection to awakening.

> In sleep, the soul acts as if it were present else-where, for its future departure in death. . . . Thus, when the body awakens, it portrays before our eyes the resurrection of the dead by returning to its natural functions. There you have the natural explanation and the rational nature of sleep. Thus, by the image of death, you are introduced to faith, you nourish hope, you learn both how to live and die, you learn watchfulness when you are asleep.[2]

There is mystery in the unknown. On his deathbed Henry Ward Beecher, scholar, expositor, and preacher

[2]Tertullian, *On the Soul* 43.11-12.

in America's early years, turned to a friend and said, "Ah . . . now the mystery."

Some people who have had a near-death experience report seeing a great white, warm, attractive light at the end of a long tunnel. Others report seeing angels at the foot of their beds, waiting to take them home.

Houdini, the world's greatest magician, promised to return from the grave if at all possible. To this day his followers gather on certain days, at certain times, awaiting his return—in vain.

HUMOR HELPS US PONDER DEATH

Because the subject is so serious, it is not surprising that people have also dealt with death through humor. For example, there was the boy who returned from church after hearing the minister preach on the topic of death—that we came from dust and will return to it. Later that day, the boy came running from his room, very excited, shouting to his mother, "Someone's under my bed, but I can't tell if they're coming or going!"

Another story tells of a funeral where the minister was giving an eloquent eulogy of the deceased. "He was the most generous man in town. His great love for his wife and family was a model for all. He was the epitome of a good citizen, husband, and father. He was a strong pillar of the church . . ." The widow turned to her daughter and said, "Go look in the casket and make sure it's your father he's talking about."

THE CHRISTIAN VIEW

There are many possible views of death, but only the Christian view offers hope for new life. For nearly two thousand years, it has provided followers of Jesus Christ with the hope of resurrection and eternal life. This view is based on Jesus' words when he said, "I am the resurrection and the life."[3] He later proved his words by his own triumph over death.

The fact of Christ's resurrection is a nonnegotiable of the Christian faith. Part of the ancient creed that Christians have repeated through the centuries is this: Christ "was crucified, died, and was buried. On the third day he rose again. He ascended into heaven, and is seated at the right hand of the Father." And because Christ lives, his followers also shall live after death.

The apostle Paul wrote to the church at Corinth that in Christ's sacrifice for us and resurrection there is the assurance of resurrection and eternal life for all who believe in him. The essence of the good news, and the meaning of Christ's resurrection from death, is given by John in his Gospel: "For God loved the world so much that he gave his only Son so that anyone who

[3]John 11:25, New International Version.

believes in him shall not perish but have eternal life."[4]

That is the promise to all who believe. In the Christian view, death is like the chrysalis that shrouds the larva of a butterfly, and resurrection is like the butterfly emerging in all its glory.

MOVING ON

In April of last year, I received a telephone call from my friend Dr. McGavran. His wife had been close to death for some time. He had faithfully sat by her bedside, holding her hand, as she passed in and out of a coma. When death finally came, Dr. McGavran called to tell me, not that his wife had died, but that she had "moved on," an accurate description of those who die in Christ.

A month later we recorded Dr. McGavran for our video *Live Long and Love It*. He spoke these words:

> To many people, death is simply the ending of life. I was wide awake yesterday, I am dead today, and I will be buried tomorrow . . . that's the belief of so many people.
>
> That's not my belief. I believe that when the body dies, it is just like taking off an old garment. A person in Christ will be called home to

---

[4]Corinthians 15; John 3:16, The Living Bible.

live in everlasting peace and joy and strength and gladness. They will be with their Savior Jesus Christ, and with all their friends and relatives who have gone on before them. I believe there is a great life awaiting beyond the gates of heaven; and I look forward moment by moment, day by day, month by month, year by year to being received at the gates of that city.

But when you have hope in Jesus Christ, hope in the future life, hope in the calling of God, then you are filled with feelings of possibility as you walk forward knowing that God is God, we are his children, and we are going to walk in abundant life as God wants us to walk, with great joy, with great peace, and great power.

As I reach the age of ninety-two and wonder what life has yet in store for me, I suddenly realize that the Lord has called me and blessed me with eternal life and that when I die, I am not going to be entombed in some earthly grave and disappear; I am going to be taken up to heaven and walk through those gates where I will meet my relatives and all my fellow Christians—the men and women whom I have known all my life will be there to greet me and take me to the throne where I will meet my Savior and Lord.

On July 10, 1990, three months after his wife's death, Dr. Donald A. McGavran "moved on"—a transition he was eagerly anticipating.

TALKING ABOUT DEATH

As I said earlier, if one chooses to deal with it openly and honestly, death doesn't have to have the last word. So let's have a cup of tea together and talk.

I recommend that you contact your clergyperson, ask him to come by your home, and tell him you want to talk about life after death. One of the early questions you should ask is whether he has the assurance of eternal life. If the answer is yes, ask how he knows. If the answer is no, thank him for coming, but don't waste your time or his.

How does one have assurance that death does not have the last word, and how does one prepare for this moving on? Intelligent people today prepare wills and make other necessary arrangements to care for their earthly treasure. Yet so often these same people—intelligent people, nice people—fail to make the necessary preparation for their "heavenly estate." How foolish a person would be not to be able to answer Jesus' probing question: "What profit is there if you gain the whole world—and lose eternal life?"[5]

[5]Matthew 16:26, *The Living Bible.*

YOUR PREPARATION

May I talk with you about your preparation for this heavenly estate? You will understand if I quote from the Bible, for Scripture holds the key to successfully moving on.

The theme of redemption (God's means of providing eternal life for those who choose to respond) runs throughout Scripture. It begins in the very early pages of the Old Testament with the promise of the Messiah. With the coming of Christ, as the New Testament records, God's promise is fulfilled.

But, you ask, why is this redemption necessary? Scripture points out, and we know from our own experience, that "all have sinned; all fall short of God's glorious ideal; yet now God declares us 'not guilty' of offending him if we trust in Jesus Christ, who in his kindness freely takes away our sins."[6]

Another Scripture speaks of our inherent sin: "We—every one of us—have strayed away like sheep! We, who left God's paths to follow our own. Yet God laid on him [Christ] the guilt and sins of every one of us!"[7] Scripture reveals that Jesus Christ has taken our sin upon himself, and he has paid our penalty. We have forgiveness from God as we, by faith, receive Jesus Christ as our personal Lord and Savior, and

[6]Romans 3:23, *The Living Bible.*   [7]Isaiah 53:6, *The Living Bible.*

accept his death as payment for our sin.

He came to pay a debt he didn't owe because we owed a debt we couldn't pay.

How do you receive Christ? In simple childlike faith, ask forgiveness for your sins, and ask Jesus Christ to become your Lord and Savior.

Can a person work his or her way into heaven? According to Scripture, the answer is no. "For it is by grace you have been saved, through faith—and this is not from yourselves, it is the gift of God—not by works, so that no one can boast."[8]

Is it ever too late to seek God's forgiveness? Yes, after one has moved on. "Now is the day of salvation."[9]

GOD'S PROMISE

What is God's promise to those who believe, those who are his children by faith?

"I will never, never reject them."[10]

"I will not abandon you or leave you as orphans."[11]

"Let not your heart be troubled. You are trusting God, now trust in me. There are many

---

[8]Ephesians 2:8-9, New International Version. [9]2 Corinthians 6:2b, New International Version. [10]John 6:37b, *The Living Bible.* [11]John 14:18, *The Living Bible.*

homes up there where my Father lives, and I am going to prepare them for your coming. When everything is ready, then I will come and get you, so that you can always be with me where I am. If this weren't so, I would tell you plainly. And you know where I am going and how to get there."

"No, we don't," Thomas said. "We haven't any idea where you are going, so how can we know the way?"

Jesus told him, "I am the Way—yes, and the Truth and the Life. No one can get to the Father except by means of me."[12]

AS WE PART . . .

But perhaps you are not ready to move on. You may identify with the mother in this story told by her son:

Some time ago my mother, now ninety-six years old, was instructing me on what she wanted done when she went "south of town" (the location of the cemetery, and the way she refers to her own death). As she talked on I interrupted: "It sounds like you have every-thing prepared."

[12]John 14:1-6, *The Living Bible.*

"Yes," she replied. "There's only one thing I haven't yet done."

"What's that?" I asked.

"I haven't set the date."[13]

In these pages we have laughed together and we have learned together. We have progressed in our knowledge and understanding of the best years of our lives.

My challenge to you, as we part, is to live and enjoy life to its very fullest. Keep adding exciting pieces to your life mosaic. Live with courage. Make healthy choices. Envision a new dream and go for it. Build humor into every day. Fight back! Stretch your limits. Love. And as a result, live long and love it!

My greatest hope is that you have found—or that you will find—a meaningful faith in Jesus Christ. Your faith will not only give you a view of eternity full of hope and love, but it will enrich your days here as well. May those days be productive and rewarding for you in the areas that really count in life.

Thank you for allowing me to spend time with

[13]*Senior Tidings* (Minneapolis: Evangelical Free Church, Church Ministries Department), September 1990, 13.

you. If you've found this book to be helpful, give it to a friend. And then model for your friend those special characteristics of people who live long and love it.

My best to you,

DISCUSSION QUESTIONS

1. Write a one-paragraph statement of your view of death and what might follow. If you are part of a group, have all participants write statements and discuss them together.

2. Have a person in the group reread Dr. McGavran's statement on death. Discuss.

3. What steps should be taken now to prepare oneself for eternal life?

L.I.F.E.
INTERNATIONAL

WHAT IS L.I.F.E. INTERNATIONAL?

L.I.F.E. is a Christian club for seniors who want to "live in full effectiveness." A L.I.F.E. club meets between two and four times a month. Activities and general themes at club gatherings include Christian enrichment study, service and ministry activities, relationship-building times, recreational events, educational "safaris," and information from leaders in various fields of interest to seniors.

WHO PARTICIPATES IN L.I.F.E.?

L.I.F.E. is open to anyone fifty-five years or older who has an attitude that retirement is not the beginning of "winter," but the beginning of "harvest." These people see the coming years as providing an opportunity to serve Christ and his church. They feel they can make a contribution through their experience, knowledge, skills, energy, and resources.

L.I.F.E.ers are individuals who want to keep growing and discovering. They recognize that volunteering, particularly for Christian service, is increasingly a way of life for millions of senior church members. Those who participate in L.I.F.E. are people looking for places where their skills and compassion are needed, people who have been set free from work to become productive. The L.I.F.E. club is a means of joining with other people in this pursuit.

HOW DOES A CHURCH GET A L.I.F.E. CLUB STARTED?

A L.I.F.E. information kit is available for a small fee. It includes twenty-five flyers for recruiting prospective club members, a booklet on how to organize and charter a L.I.F.E. club, a forty-five-minute color video for use in the initial L.I.F.E. club meeting, a church member survey form and instructions for analysis, guidelines for gathering information on the senior adult population in your church area, an application for a L.I.F.E. club charter, and more.

L.I.F.E. has also produced a ten-week study entitled "Live Long and Love It" which uses this book as a text. Videotapes, training seminars, consultation, and additional resource support are available to churches through this organization.

FOR MORE INFORMATION, WRITE OR PHONE:

L.I.F.E. International, 1857 Highland Oaks Drive Arcadia, CA 91006   *Telephone:*1-800-423-4844